Louis A. Banks

A Year's Prayer-Meeting Talks

Louis A. Banks

A Year's Prayer-Meeting Talks

ISBN/EAN: 9783337284695

Printed in Europe, USA, Canada, Australia, Japan

Cover: Foto ©Lupo / pixelio.de

More available books at **www.hansebooks.com**

A YEAR'S . . ..
PRAYER-MEETING
TALKS

By
REV. LOUIS ALBERT BANKS, D.D.

Author of . . .
"Christ and His Friends"
"Anecdotes and Morals"
Etc., Etc.

Funk & Wagnalls Company
NEW YORK AND LONDON

To My Friend
And One of my Prayer-Meeting Saints
THE REV. A. R. PALMER
Of Cleveland, Ohio

This Volume

is lovingly dedicated by the Author

AUTHOR'S PREFACE.

For several years I have been in receipt of letters from ministers in different parts of the country, of wide variety of denomination, suggesting that I put out a volume such as the one here presented. I have always had the pleasure and blessing of a large and interesting prayer-meeting. For many years in downtown city churches the prayer-meeting has always numbered hundreds of attendants. I think one of the chief reasons for this is that I have made much of the prayer-meeting in my announcements on Sunday, have never allowed anything to keep me away from it, and have made as careful preparation for it in the prayer-meeting talk, in the selection and arrangement of music, and indeed in all particulars, as for the services on Sunday. These prayer-meeting talks were delivered in the First Methodist Episcopal church, Cleveland, of which I am pastor, during the past year. They were dictated to my stenographer, usually on prayer-meeting morning, and always before the time of delivery. I give them forth to

Author's Preface.

my brethren with the prayer and hope that in suggestive and illustrative material they may be of service and blessing.

LOUIS ALBERT BANKS.

CLEVELAND, October 2, 1899.

CONTENTS.

	PAGE.
I.—THE CHARACTERISTICS OF A GOOD CHURCH MEMBER,	1
II.—CHRIST'S BUILDERS,	7
III.—THE UNUSED DIPLOMAS OF LIFE,	15
IV.—STRENGTH ADORNED BY LOVE,	20
V.—PROVOKING ONE ANOTHER TO GOOD WORKS,	27
VI.—THE ROAD THAT LEADS HOME,	33
VII.—CHRIST'S MISSION TO DEAF EARS,	39
VIII.—THE SOLDIER'S HOME-COMING,	44
IX.—HOW TO GET EVERYTHING YOU WANT,	50
X.—THE SPIRITUAL FARMER,	57
XI.—CHRIST'S KINGDOM OF CHARACTER,	64
XII.—RELIGIOUS GADDERS,	71
XIII.—HOW TO BECOME MORE TRULY RELIGIOUS,	75
XIV.—THE WORSHIP OF THE HEART,	80
XV.—THE KIND OF HOLINESS PLEASING TO GOD.	85
XVI.—THE ANGELS PECULIAR TO SUMMER-TIME.	90
XVII.—THE DEVILS PECULIAR TO SUMMER-TIME.	96
XVIII.—DISAGREEABLE CHRISTIANS,	101
XIX.—THE SOURCE OF OUR LOVE FOR CHRIST.	106
XX.—HOW TO KEEP CHEERFUL,	111
XXI.—THE IMPERISHABLE MAN WITHIN.	117
XXII.—THE ART OF RECEIVING GOOD ADVICE,	122
XXIII.—THE BLESSINGS OF HOPE,	128
XXIV.—WALKING WITH GOD,	132
XXV.—SPIRITUAL CULTURE,	138
XXVI.—THE GOOD AND THE BAD WORLDLINESS,	141

Contents.

	PAGE
XXVII.—The Evolution of the Shirk,	146
XXVIII.—Homesickness,	151
XXIX.—My Gospel,	156
XXX.—Making the Most of Things,	161
XXXI.—How Not to Want Everything,	167
XXXII.—Every-Day Life Made Easy,	174
XXXIII.—The Selection of Clothing for the Soul,	179
XXXIV.—The Spiritual Cupboard,	185
XXXV.—The Duty and Privilege of Forgiving Those Who Injure Us,	190
XXXVI.—Commonplace Heroes,	197
XXXVII.—The Odd Sparrow,	203
XXXVIII.—The Mountain of the Giants,	208
XXXIX.—The Special Value of Average People,	215
XL.—Christ's Philosophy of Comfort,	221
XLI.—How to Make the Bible a Personal Book,	225
XLII.—Juicy Christians,	231
XLIII.—Sleepy Christians and Their Gentle Lord,	236
XLIV.—The Power of Personal Influence,	241
XLV.—The Living Bread,	245
XLVI.—How to Get Rid of Fear,	250
XLVII.—The Taming of the Greatest Shrew in the World,	255
XLVIII.—The Divine Side of a Revival,	260
XLIX.—The Human Side of a Revival,	267
L.—What Happens When There Is a Revival of Religion,	273
LI.—A Great Revival and What Caused It.	279
LII.—The First Christmas Gifts,	284

A YEAR'S PRAYER-MEETING TALKS.

I.

THE CHARACTERISTICS OF A GOOD CHURCH MEMBER.

2 Kings x. 15.

JEHU was a dashing man who did things on the spur of the moment. It was touch and go with him every time. He was such a wild driver that it was a proverb in the country if a man was a little reckless with horses that he drove like Jehu. One man makes his mark in one way, and one in another, and this proverb about Jehu has lasted over until our time. But there was a great deal of human nature about Jehu, and this incident makes a very interesting little picture for a brief study. Jehu had been secretly anointed king and was seeking to settle himself well in the saddle of government before his enemies could get together to organize opposition to him. In this mood he was naturally suspicious of everybody and constantly on his guard. As he drove on the road he saw Jehonadab coming to meet him. Now Jehonadab was a man of the highest repute for righteousness and honor. He was a quiet man who did not take much active interest in the rough politics of his time, yet he was pleased with Jehu's coming to the kingdom, and of his own accord was on his way to tell the young king so. But Jehu did not know this, and we can see him as he checks his foaming horses for a moment, throwing them back on their haunches, and looks with flashing eyes deep into the eyes of Jehonadab, seeking to read his very soul; and his words cut like a sword, "Is thine heart right, as my heart is with thy heart?" It is steel flashing against steel, and Jehonadab looks him back straight in the eyes, look for look, and answers, "It is." Then we see the smile on Jehu's face as he bends over and stretches out his hand and cries, "If it be, give me thine hand." He lifts him up into the chariot beside him, the whip cracks, and away through the dust of the highway dash the restless horses.

Life may well be compared to a chariot-race, it is so swift and passes away so soon; and it is proper, I think, that at a time like this we should earnestly consider some of the characteristics of a good church member. In the first place, this is supremely a matter of the heart. No man or woman ever yet fulfilled his or her obligations in the Christian church unless the heart was in it. Our religion requires the intellect, too; but the heart rules the head. Hence the first question to ask of any one coming into the church is, "Is thy heart right?" Is your heart with the church? is your sympathy and your affection there?

The first thing in becoming a Christian is the giving of the heart to Christ. Whole-hearted enthusiasm will atone for multitudes of blunders of the head. If you have given your heart to Christ and his church, then your hand and the personal confession of your whole life ought to follow.

A good church member must so far as possible attend the services of his church. When Jehu was certain of Jehonadab's loyalty, he took him up into the chariot with him. He knew that Jehonadab had a good name everywhere. It wasn't a very pretty name, but it stood for honor, and faithful dealing, and a pure life. He wanted the influence of that name and personality on his side. So if you have given your heart to Christ, and he has forgiven your sins, and the church has received you into its membership and given you the right to represent it, you should honor the church by being present at its meeting and giving it everywhere all your influence. I have never seen a large Christian church that was not weakened by some people who gave it only casual attendance. The people whom the pastor counts on, and relies upon, as a general does upon tried and veteran soldiers, are those whom he knows he can be sure will be present whenever it is possible at the regular services of the church.

A good church member must have a willing spirit to help. There are always some people who have to be handled with gloves at arm's length, or they get huffy or miffed about something. The late Dr. Gumbart, of Boston, a good Baptist preacher, invented what he called "the miff tree." Up in that old, gaunt, leafless tree he had sitting about the glum and gruesome birds whose corns had been trodden on, or whose feelings had been hurt, or their sensitive feathers ruffled until they had flown up into the miff tree, and would no longer sing in the choir, or pray in the prayer-meeting, or help in the social work of the church. For your soul's sake give the "miff tree" a wide berth. If anything occurs to hurt you, go at once straight to the person interested and have an understanding. Life is too short, and the great work which Christ has called you to do is far too important, to allow yourself to become useless in the church on account of any little thing of that sort. Don't wait for a big office. If you could only know of how much value the people are who are ready to take hold and help, if it's only to wash dishes or sell tickets, you would be grateful to be so useful in the Lord's vineyard.

A good church member must be generous to share according to his ability in supporting the church. The church doesn't do much for you unless it enters into your affections sufficiently to make you willing to give of your money to help on its prosperity. A religion that stops short of a man's pocketbook hasn't got a very deep hold on him yet. Don't make the mistake of imagining that you are not under obligations to give because you are only able to give a small amount. The obligation is just as strong on you to give the twenty-five cents which you are able to contribute, as it is on another man to give the twenty-five dollars which is his rightful share. It may not look so large in the eyes of men, but we know from what Jesus said of the poor woman who cast in her two mites, that it does not lose in the comparison in the eyes of our Savior. A stingy, miserly member of the church is never happy in the church. How could he be? His conscience prods him all the time; he feels so mean that he imagines everybody else is as mean as he feels. On the other hand, the most charitable, kindly, gracious, and happy spirits in the church that I have ever had anything to do with, have been those who have given liberally according to their means. God loves the cheerful giver, and the love of God is the sweetest atmosphere that can pervade any man's life.

A good church member holds his church and its good name and prosperity as sacred as the apple of his eye. He is always ready to stand up for it and defend it wherever he goes. He is ever seeking to bring credit to it, and to so live that his own life will reflect honor upon his church. He is careful about the reputation of his brethren, knowing that in a church, as in the human body, one member can not suffer without bringing some shadow upon all; and that, on the other hand, honor can not come to any member of the church without reflecting something of its light and glory upon all.

II.
CHRIST'S BUILDERS.

Matthew vii. 24-27 (Rev. Ver.).

WE are all builders. Our thoughts, our emotions, our words, our actions are constantly working away at a house not made with hands, builded of imperishable soul fabric. The most important house in the world is that which we call character. Better to live in one small room of a tenement-house with the body, while the soul dwells in a mansion of integrity and righteousness with many windows that open into the realm of spiritual beauty, than to live in the most splendid dwelling in the city, on the most fashionable street, with all the pomp and splendor of earthly show, while the soul dwells in a dark and dismal cellar without light or hope.

Every one of us is building his own house. In building our modern city houses, if a man have the money he can let the contract to a builder to construct him a house on a certain plan, and go his way and trouble himself no more about it until the house is done. But one cannot build by proxy in the construction of character. It is a personal affair, and must be built day after day and year after year by the personal strokes of our own hammer. It is a continuous thing. A man is all his lifetime building it. One can not build up a good character, and then go off and do what he pleases and come home to find it just the same as when he left. Yet that is what some people seem to think. They act as tho they thought because they were converted thirty or forty years ago and built up a certain religious experience and character, that that is all that is necessary. There could not be a greater mistake. This house of the soul is building all our lives, and can never be left to take care of itself. We must work steadily on until the last. "He that endureth to the end shall be saved." As Dr. Parkhurst wittily says, there is nothing in God's earth that grows rank and fetid sooner than an experience. Our hymn asks, "Where is the blessedness I knew when first I saw the Lord?" Don't know; and it wouldn't do you any good if you had it; blessedness doesn't keep. It is one of the all-pervading principles that the more delicate a thing is and the more finely organized, the more directly it will decay and fall to pieces when once it has been parted from the root it sprang from. The perfume will evaporate from the rose, and the petals fall off very soon after it has left the stalk. Strayed or stolen—a religious experience! The hymn just quoted from is an advertisement for lost joy that has jumped the fence and gone loose. It is like hunting after the blaze of a lamp when the oil is all burnt out. Keep the wick trimmed and the lamp filled, and you will have blaze enough without advertising for last night's blaze—you do not know where that is, and could make nothing of it even if you did. Now, there is a lot of meaning in all this, and it lies right down at the level of our exigency. Good things have got to be made over and over and everlastingly reduplicated. The fresh river must incessantly draw on the young rivulets that incessantly trickle from the hillside. Christian joy that does not bear the stamp of this very day and date is a Silurian deposit, an evangelical relic, piety fossilized.

And our whole house of character is like that. What is past, of course, has to do with the present. If we did good work yesterday, it is easier to do good work to-day, and that will make it still easier for to-morrow. But because the house was pleasant and beautiful until yesterday does not prevent us from putting untempered mortar in the wall to-day. Taken in a reverent sense, it is absolutely true that life is what we make it.

Jesus says that every one who hears his words,

every one who comes to know his divine message, will build a house of conduct, and that every such house will be tested. The wind will blow upon it, the rain will beat against it, and no such house, no matter by whom constructed, will escape a thorough testing in every part. There is no basis whatever in the Bible for the delusive dream that is proclaimed in some quarters to-day, that it is possible for a Christian to reach such a state of ecstatic holiness that he will be beyond the danger of temptation. There is no such promise as that in the Bible. And every illustration God has given us of the history of those who have sought to build up characters pleasing to him speaks to us of the universal struggle and battle with the storm. Depend upon it, your house will be tried by the wind and drenched by the rain. The temptations that come from the assaults of the enemy of our souls and from the deep sorrows that sweep over us are as real and terrible to-day as at any time in the history of the world. Longfellow, in that pathetic poem, "The Chamber Over the Gate," recording David's grief over Absalom, says:

> "There is no far or near,
> There is neither there nor here,
> There is neither soon nor late,
> In that Chamber over the Gate;

Nor any long ago
To that cry of human wo,
O Absalom, my son!"

When we touch the deep sorrows and temptations of life, we find that we are close kin to those who sorrowed and struggled with temptation thousands of years ago. And when we would know the way of victory we must go to Him who was tempted in all points like as we are, yet without sin. That story of Christ's temptation never seemed so real to me as in reading recently Dr. Alexander Macleod's translation of it into a more modern form: A young man might have been seen one day, faint and weary, in a wild desert and among wild beasts in an Eastern land. He was exhausted with hunger, and the marks of it were on his face. Poor and haggard and hungry tho he looked, he was the son of a king and was on the way to his kingdom. The wonderful thing was, that it was his father who sent him into the desert and suffered him to be without food for many days. A still more wonderful thing was, that when he was suffering the sharpest pangs of hunger and ready to perish, he did not doubt his father's love, nor that his father's way of bringing him to his kingdom was the best.

But one day a stranger came up to him and said: "You are the son of that king of whom everybody has heard, and to whom this wilderness belongs. If you be his son, why should you remain hungry? Bid the wilderness provide a table for you. Turn these stones into bread." Now, this young man could actually have turned the stones into bread. That would have satisfied his hunger. That might save his life. That was a way which at the moment might have seemed right. His father had sent him into the wilderness; his father had sent him hunger instead of bread; and he knew his father to be wise and good and loving. "No," he said to the stranger, "I will follow my father to the end, trust him to the end, trust him through hunger and faintness, trust him even to death. My father's love is better to me than bread." This stranger was a very deceitful man; but he saw at a glance that the king's son was resolved to go forward on the path of trust. So he followed the young man until he came to the capital town of the kingdom, and by and by they went up to the high towers of the temple. "It is a great thing," said the stranger, once more, "to be a king's son, and especially the king's son you are. Your father cares for you every moment, and would not suffer a hair of your head to be hurt. His servants follow you, watch over you, care for you. Suppose—since you are cared for in this way, as the king's son—you cast yourself down to the court below. See, there is a whole army ready to receive you in their arms!" The young man simply said: "To trust my father's care when I am in the way of obedience and duty is one thing; to put it to the test in the way you propose, if I disbelieved it, is another. It would be tempting my father. And it is written, Thou shalt not tempt the King."

So the stranger saw how noble this youth was, and how kingly and well-fitted to reign. And he took him to a high mountain, and showed him all its glory and the glory of all the kingdoms on the earth, and said: "All these will I give unto thee, if thou wilt love me and trust me as thou lovest and trusteth thy father." But the young man turned round upon him in anger, and said: "Get thee behind me! For it is written, Thou shalt worship the Lord thy God, and him only shalt thou serve." Then the stranger left him. And the heavens opened and "angels came and ministered unto him"; and the smile of the Father shone round about him like a great light; and far up in the depths of heaven there were songs of victory. For this was none other than the Son of God, and the stranger was the devil who sought to lead him out of the right way.

From this story of the obedience of Christ to his Father we may see the essence of that solid foundation upon which we may build a character that will stand through all the storms of temptation which shall beat upon it. Jesus says: "Every one therefore which heareth these words of mine, and doeth them, shall be likened unto a wise man, which built his house upon a rock." It is clear that the rock which Jesus sets forth as a safe foundation for our house of human life is that of obedience to him. It is the doer of the word upon whom the storms shall beat in vain. He will take care of those who in obedient humility do his will.

III.
THE UNUSED DIPLOMAS OF LIFE.

John vi. 12.

SOMETIMES at first glance, or at superficial glance, there seems to be a great waste in human life. It was once my pleasant fortune to be entertained in a beautiful farm home in the outskirts of one of the quaint old Dutch towns of the upper Hudson. The matronly woman who came to meet me was stately and gracious, but had an atmosphere that told of the chastening of sorrow. After a little, when she showed me to my room, as she opened the door into a beautiful chamber she said with a lowering of her voice, and a sort of indefinable lingering of tone, as tho she were talking of sacred things: "I am going to give you the room that was my daughter's, who is now in heaven. Everything in it is just as it was when she left it. The books are on the shelves, the pictures hanging on the walls, the vases and photographs on the mantel—even the arrangement of the chairs and the furniture in the room is just the same as when she went away."

Then she stepped across the room to a beautiful old-fashioned bookcase, and pointing through the glass door to a rolled parchment tied with a pretty pink ribbon, she said: "And there is her diploma, lying just as she threw it there, when she came home from college, but a few days before she was taken ill. I came up with her to the room, and she flung the diploma in there with a sort of girlish glee, and it stuck at an angle, that way, across the compartment of the bookcase. She closed the door on it and said, ' Well, I'm glad I've got you, anyhow!' and it has never been touched since. Two weeks later, we went with her over to the cemetery and laid her beside her father; and there lies her unused diploma that cost her so much hard work, and that she was so proud to obtain."

The conversation impressed me very deeply, and that unused diploma gave me many an hour of hard thinking that night. I saw that the dear old mother had a painful feeling that there had somehow been a great waste in all the hard work her daughter had performed to obtain this diploma, which represented an education that she was not permitted to use on earth; and I could not sleep until I had settled the problem in my own mind as to whether her view was the correct one. The more I thought about it, the more clearly it seemed to me that this case, tho rather unique in its conditions, was like a great many others that are happening to young and old all the time. People are all the while acquiring knowledge or discipline which they never seem to have any opportunity of using. Many people hesitate to pay the price in sacrifice and hard work to enlarge their scope of wisdom, for fear they will never have any opportunity to get special returns for it in dollars and cents. The interrogation-point that stands like a ghost in the path of many a boy or girl on the way to college is the question, "Will it pay?"

Very often a farmer or mechanic says: "If my boy were going to be a preacher or a lawyer or a doctor, or my girl expected to be a musician or a teacher, it might be well enough to send them to college; but if they are going to be farmers, or builders, or bankers, or housekeepers, they will never have a chance to use a college education, and it is only a waste of time and money."

It is not a question whether a wider education will make the boy or girl a money-getter; the greater question is, Will it make a larger, nobler man or woman? Will it arouse and give wings to a great imaginative soul, so that instead of seeing in human life simply a mass of strugglers, like so many larger human ants in an exaggerated ant-hill, they will see with the vision of God, and realize that in every human soul with which they come in contact there is a mighty battle going on, and that every human heart is interesting in its thought, its joy and sorrow, and that nothing human can ever be commonplace?

A good many boys and girls in these days are tempted (and some of the schools are likely to advise them that way) to prepare themselves simply to be specialists in what is to be the main work of their lives. Of course, up to a certain point, this is all right; but the trouble is, that if it is carried to excess we have lawyers who are simply patent, or marine, or criminal lawyers; we have doctors who are physicians to the eye, or the ear, or the lungs; we have machinists who know how to make one wheel or polish one spring in a watch, and every other part of their brain seems to dry and wither up. It seems to me that to-day we need all-around men. But whatever calling or profession you choose, let the young people remember that a lawyer, or doctor, or preacher, or teacher, or blacksmith, or housekeeper, or clerk should be something more than that: they should first of all be cultivated, Christian men and women. The more generous the education of mind and heart, the greater personalities they will be, not only in their chosen line of business by which they earn their bread and butter, but in the larger relations which they will have to the world.

No honest work which we do to enlarge our scope of knowledge, to quicken and clarify our mental or spiritual vision, so that the mountains, the forests, the gardens and fields, as well as human faces and hearts, become more interesting books to us, revealing the goodness and the glory of God, can ever possibly be wasted.

Even in a case like that of the young girl with which we started, her unused diploma was by no means wasted. We are sure that in heaven intelligence, educated imagination, trained habits of fidelity, and disciplined patience must be as valuable qualities and as highly honored as here on earth. Honesty will still be honesty, fidelity will still pass as current coin, patience will still wait upon God with his approval, and faith and hope and love will still abide victoriously in any world to which God shall take his trusting and loving children.

Let us go on gathering all the knowledge and cultivation of mind and heart that we can, for we may be sure that He who used the little fisher-lad's loaves of bread and string of fish in feeding the multitude, and was careful to have all the fragments gathered up after the feast, will not let any beautiful or useful information or art we have acquired or won go to waste.

IV.
STRENGTH ADORNED BY LOVE.

Solomon's Song viii. 6.

THE paragraph to which these sentences form the open door is one of those literary gems with which the Bible abounds. It is the appeal of love for preeminence, its argument for being given the chief place. In all the literature of love there is not a more splendid or majestic passage. "Set me as a seal upon thine heart, as a seal upon thine arm: for love is strong as death; jealousy is cruel as the grave: the coals thereof are coals of fire which hath a most vehement flame. Many waters can not quench love; neither can the floods drown it. If a man would give all the substance of his house for love, it would utterly be contemned."

If we take this to be a literal love-story, we have a woman asking her kingly lover to have her name or likeness stamped upon her beloved's heart and arm: on his breast above his heart as the seat of affection, and on his arm where it might be constantly in view. There is suggested the desire of every loving heart to be kept in tender remembrance by the one who is the object of its love. Love must have love in return. There is a suggestion, also, of a fear that love might be diminished by distance, especially where it may have rivals. Love trembles at the thought of the proverb proving true, "Out of sight, out of mind." And so to be set as a seal upon the breast and arm, as a reminder of the deathless character of her affection, and of the preciousness of a love which all the wealth of Solomon could not have bought, and which could only be repaid by his love in return, is the request which is made by this devoted soul.

Surely we do no violence to Scripture if we spiritualize this beautiful incident. It is in harmony with the spirit of God's revelation to us concerning his love for us in Jesus Christ and our love for him, which is aroused in return. John says concerning our love for Christ that "we love him because he first loved us." The great sacrifice of Christ in our behalf, the love that saw us in our sins, and put aside the glory of heaven to come down to earth and suffer and die in our stead, is surely a love which can never be repaid except by love itself.

This Scripture suggests to me another meaning, however, which is very comforting to my own heart, and which I hope may comfort us all. The arm is the symbol of strength and power, and when a trusting woman asks to be set as a seal upon her beloved's arm, does it not mean that the strength of that arm is pledged for her protection? A seal in those old days was used in the place of a signature to a deed, or a compact of the most sacred kind. To be set as a seal upon the arm of a strong king like Solomon meant that the power of the great king was pledged for the defense of the woman who loved him. She may have been as weak as the vine clinging to the giant tree, but all the strength of the king became hers if the seal of this sacred compact was set upon his strong arm.

If we set upon this story the seal of the Spirit, then this can only suggest to us the splendid strength of Christian character. And the Christian, if he be true and genuine, is the strongest, most forceful human character in the world, inasmuch as goodness is stronger than evil, purity stronger than vice, sobriety stronger than drunkenness, peace stronger than strife, joy more forceful than sorrow. Inasmuch as love is stronger than hate, or indeed God stronger than the devil, so much greater is the strength and forcefulness of true Christian character than any personality a wicked world can present. And the character which is presented by Christ, and by Paul, as the ideal

Christian character, is ever a strong, forceful personality. The manliness of Jesus and Paul stand out as models of the strength of the noblest chivalry. Christians can not be weaklings. We must be "good soldiers of Jesus Christ."

And yet it is still another thought upon which I wish to put the emphasis in our study at this time. This loving woman was not satisfied at a compact which gave her all the strength of Solomon's kingdom; that might satisfy an ambitious adventuress, but it could never satisfy a sincerely loving heart. She longed for something more than that, and so makes her appeal, "Set me as a seal upon thine heart." If we shall spiritualize that, we shall understand the poet who sings:

"Set me as a seal upon thine arm,
  On that mighty place of mighty strength,
  For all other arms to dust, at length,
    Turn, dear Lord.

"Set me as a seal upon thine heart,
  On that mighty place of mighty love,
  For all other hearts must cease to move,
    But thine, dear Lord.

"And thus ever on thine arm and heart,
  In a covenant thou canst not break,
  Thou'lt remember, tho I sleep or wake,
    I am thine, dear Lord."

If we are thus set as a seal upon the heart of Christ, we shall not only have the strength of his mighty arm to sustain us in the hour of weakness and temptation, but we shall be adorned with the beauty of his love, and the sweetness of his sympathy and tenderness shall be given to us. We shall not only be strong in goodness and justice and truth, but these great qualities will be beautified by love.

And is not that the great need of the world today? Is it not the crying need of all civilization that we shall have great characters, strong to do and dare and achieve, but whose strength shall be softened and beautified by the gentleness of Jesus Christ? We are living in a time when strong men abound. There are more giants in these days than at any time in the history of the world. Men spring up on every side who have the genius to seize hold of the mighty forces of nature, and master them, and make them their servants. In iron, and coal, and oil, and gas, and electricity, and indeed every elemental force of the world in which we live, men are rising up to seize with strong arm, and to control and master them for their own good, and, incidentally, if not otherwise, for the good of humanity.

We hear an immense deal of talk in our time about corporations and trusts, and we see in this multiplication of wealth opportunities for the great aggregation of wealth into a few hands, until some people are frightened and can see only ruin in the outlook. Is it not, after all, the old struggle of the centuries after power?—and the result must depend altogether on how the power is used. We do not care how strong a man is if his strength is controlled and adorned by love. If his strength is governed by selfishness, then evil will come from his power.

If all strong men had the spirit of Jesus Christ, there would surely be no crying out against great strength in single hands. Christ exercised the most marvelous power over nature and over human life. If he had used his strength to speak into being storms that would sweep away villages and shipwreck the boats of the fisherman, he would have been a man of terror. But when he used his power to speak the taunting waves into quiet with his words of "Peace, be still," his power was a benediction and not a threat. If he had used his power to make men deaf, or blind, or lame, or dumb, or to bewitch them with demoniac spirits, what a curse his strange control over human nature would have been to the people with whom he lived! But when he went about among them opening deaf ears, causing blind eyes to see, making the lame to leap for joy, healing the lepers, dispossessing devils, and raising the dead, his every step was a blessing and his great power, so beautified by love, made him the most majestic character the world has ever seen.

V.

PROVOKING ONE ANOTHER TO GOOD WORKS.

Hebrews x. 24; 2 Corinthians ix. 2.

THIS word "provoke" as used in the Scriptures is usually on the wrong side of the ledger. It is often used throughout the Old Testament in connection with the bringing of judgment upon Israel because of their sins against God. And more than once in the New Testament Paul uses it in warning parents to such care in the treatment of their children as not to provoke in them sinful tempers. We have set before us here, however, the right kind of provoking. We have suggested the possibility of our so doing duty, and so incarnating the Christian spirit into our lives, that our character and conduct will provoke in others a desire to live the kind of life exemplified in us.

I think the only life that can possibly have that power to give fresh impulse to others must in its nature be positive and aggressive. It must not only be good, but it must be vitally and positively good. I do not mean that it must be noisily good, but that there must be about it a virile and conquering quality that will make conquest of the imagination and desire of others.

I think there has been a great deal too much emphasis put at times on what we give up for Christ. Many people just entering the Christian life, as well as those who have been Christians long enough to know better, seem to lay nearly all the emphasis of their Christian thinking on "What shall I give up for Christ?" But it seems to me, when we turn the whole matter over and look on the other side of it, and ask, "What can I *be* and *do* that will best show my love for Christ?" there is no trouble about answering the first question. There is no virtue in simply giving up things. We need to take up the Christian character and life with such devotion and enthusiasm, and wear it with such love and fidelity, that we shall make it seem beautiful and attractive to the people who behold us. It is not enough that we are true and honest; we must be beautifully true and graciously honest. We are urged to live so attractively that we shall "adorn the doctrine of God our Savior in all things."

Paul suggests this possibility in the twelfth of Romans, where he says, "He that giveth, let him do it with simplicity." How many times gifts are made which are good and generous in themselves, and serve a good purpose, and yet are made with so much display, and made to so minister to egotism and pride, that they lose their best influence on the public heart, and have a tendency rather to discourage other people from giving than to provoke them to like generosity. They lack the adornment of simplicity, which is the one flower that can make giving beautiful.

Again in the same chapter Paul writes, "He that showeth mercy with cheerfulness." Did you never receive mercy from some one in such an ugly, morose way that you felt as if you wanted to slap the person who showed it? The mercy was granted in such a manner that it left a bad taste in your mouth forever afterward. It lacked the adornment, the jewel, of cheerfulness, which takes all the sting out of receiving mercy at the hands of another.

You may find another illustration in the case of the ten lepers whom Christ sent away to their cleansing. All of them were healed, but only one came back to give thanks to the Savior. There is a great deal of pathos in Christ's question, "Where are the nine?" I do not think it correct for us to say that the other nine were not thankful, or that they were frauds and had no faith; every one of them had faith enough to be healed. No, the only trouble with the other nine was this, that they did not have the gracious and beautiful spirit of thanksgiving which would have brought them back, with the one who did come, to express their gratitude to God. Are there not many who are living just the same way to-day? They believe in God, and in Christ, and in the Holy Spirit; they live prayerful, honorable lives; if it were necessary, they would go to the stake before they would renounce Jesus. Yet they do not make their lives beautiful by a constant spirit of thanksgiving, ready everywhere, in business and in social life, to give Christ grateful credit as the Source of all that is noble and sweet in character and career. And yet it is only by so completely surrendering our lives in personal devotion to Christ that these attractive graces of the spirit will by their beauty and their perfume provoke others to soul-gardening on their own account.

In living such a life, in being such a man or woman, we shall attain without difficulty the service which we ought to render to Christ. Grand Phillips Brooks never uttered a greater truth than when he said: Love utters itself in Duty, and Duty strengthens Love. If Duty grows weak, it must climb to the fountain-head of Love and drink. If Love grows doubtful and hesitates, it must lean and steady itself on the strong staff of Duty. It takes both of these to make life complete in a world in which there is no love without its duty and no duty without its love. It is a most inspiring thought, that never yet did God put any high emotion in the soul of any of his children that God's word did not instantly stand before that child with a duty in its hand, saying: "This is the task which belongs to your new impulse. Do this task, and the love shall be really yours; not merely the fleeting gleam of a passing sunbeam on your bosom, but the settled warmth of a perpetual sunshine in your heart." Never does a new love descend from heaven that a new duty does not spring out of the earth. God fills your soul with pity, and even while you think upon it some great need knocks at your door. God gives you courage, and the oppressed and neglected flee under your strong arm for protection. God gives you light, and the cloud of some ignorance rolls up out of the night demanding your daylight to cause it to flee away. Let us be in our place a Christ, and God will give us Christ's work to do in our day and time. And he will let none of our work done in this spirit be lost.

> "The look of sympathy, the gentle word,
> Spoken so low that only angels heard;
> The secret act of pure self-sacrifice,
> Unseen by men, but marked by angels' eyes—
> These are not lost.

"The happy dream that gladdened all our youth,
 When dreams had less of self and more of truth;
 The childhood's faith, so tranquil and so sweet,
 Which sat like Mary at the Master's feet—
   These are not lost.

"The kindly plan devised for others' good,
 So seldom guessed, so little understood;
 The quiet, steadfast love that strove to win
 Some wanderer from the tortuous ways of sin—
   These are not lost.

"Not lost, O Lord! For in thy city bright
 Our eyes shall see the past by clearer light;
 And things long hidden from our gaze below
 Thou wilt reveal, and we shall surely know
   These are not lost."

VI.
THE ROAD THAT LEADS HOME.

Ecclesiastes xii. 5.

MAN was not intended to be a tramp or a prisoner, but a traveler. We are pilgrims on a journey. Life ought not to be an experience in which we are dragged or driven. We should go holding the reins with a masterful hand, driving along the highway of holiness on our journey home.

It is a very simple and homely, but, I pray God, a very sweet and comforting message which I bring to you to-night. Home is a beautiful word. Sad indeed the fate of the man whose heart does not grow fonder when, as the day closes and the toil is over until to-morrow, he says, "And now I will go home." Home is a creation of the spiritual far more than of the physical. It can not be built of bricks or stone or lumber; these may furnish materials to make a temple for home, but they can not add the altar or the sacrifice or the worship of love, which gives to home its divine quality.

We make many proverbs about home. Among them is, "Home is where the heart is." When I was in San Francisco I inquired of the pastor of a great church there how to find my way by rail up to my father's place, sixty miles north of that city; and after telling me, he urged me to come back and preach for him the next Sunday, but I smiled and said, "No, I shall spend Sunday with the folks at home;" and he replied, "It seems strange to hear you talk about home in a place you never saw, and even the way to which you have just been inquiring of me." But I answered: "True I never saw it, but up there among the orchards there is a little cottage where my gray-haired father lives, who used to carry me on his back, and where my mother dwells, who used to nestle me in her arms. And about them in the orchards adjoining are the sisters that were my childhood's playmates. I think that will be home." And I found it so.

These earthly homes are types of the "long home" toward which some of you are going like tired children. I am speaking to Christians to-night, to people who are on the way home; but if any others listen who are wandering prodigals away from the Father's house, I would to God you might get homesick to-night, and start home even while we talk about it. We are assured that our

Savior is making great preparations for us in the heavenly home. I like the words which he has used to describe it. They indicate to me that our individuality is considered and every peculiar need prepared for in our "long home" to which we are going. Jesus says, "In my Father's house are many mansions." I think that sounds very aristocratic and cold to many people. I think it would help us if we would interpret it into our modern language. We use the word mansion to indicate a comfortable, roomy, well-fitted home. In some countries they call the main house on the plantation or on a great estate the mansion house. It is just a first-class home. There are many of these, Christ says, and I think that means more than multitude; it means in quality and character. Some people get the idea that heaven may be a very beautiful and stately place, but a very monotonous place, where the architecture is all alike, and the music always set to the same tune. But surely there is nothing in the Bible to indicate such a thing. There we are assured that our individuality is as marked in heaven as on earth. "One star differeth from another star in glory," Paul says, and people do not all have the same home in heaven; each man has that suited to him.

Who of us could endure having somebody else map out a heaven for us? Here is a tired man longing for rest, and with no ear for music, and the idea of heaven where he would always be in a crowd, and hear nothing but anthems by a mammoth choir, does not attract him. But there are many homes in heaven, and the tired rest there. "They rest from their labors, and their works do follow them."

But here is a man alive to his finger-tips, who just breathes in the air and thanks God every day that he is alive. Work to him is what the road is to a fleet horse that pulses on reins, which wants to be going and finds joy in endless exercise. He finds recreation is some other kind of work. It does not mean anything to such a man to tell him of a heaven of rest. There are many homes in heaven, and the man who wants to use his home only as the center of his energies, from whence he goes forth on missions of helpfulness and blessing, shall find the home to suit him.

There are many to whom heaven is a place of knowledge; the mysteries of life and death have given them many an hour of anxiety, and they have beat against the walls of silence, perplexed, and have wondered what was beyond. And they rejoice that tho now they see through a glass darkly, the time shall come when they shall see face to face, and shall know even as they are known.

Thank God that heaven is full of homes; and he who has never made two maple-trees alike, who has made a separate study of each individual human being, has a different home, congenial surroundings and fellowship and employment for every one of us in the "long home" toward which we are traveling.

Some of you have been trying all your lives to get a home to perfectly suit you; you have patched it up, put on a room here and taken down a partition there; but how few people there are who would not change their home in some way to-night, before they go to sleep, if they could do it without expense and without annoyance. We shall have a home at last which will fit us completely. Compared to the home there, all these earthly habitations are only tents and tabernacles, that will soon fall to pieces in spite of anything we can do. But don't worry, there is a home building for us that will be just large enough, just light enough, and beautiful and glorious beyond all dreams of the imagination.

We can afford to be patient since the future is so well cared for. We are like the miner who goes to the Klondike, and digs in the frozen earth and lives in a tent or a cabin with an ice floor, and suffers untold hardships because he feels that he is making sure the future comfort and peace of his home. If a man can find such courage and inspiration in the hope of security for so brief a period, what a well-spring of courage should we find in the assurance of Jesus that our future in heaven is in his own dear hand. It ought to make us strong to bear and do for the brief period of earthly hardships and sacrifices that may be required of us.

"Be strong to hope, O heart!
   Tho day is bright,
The stars can only shine
   In the dark night.
Be strong, O heart of mine!
   Look toward the light.

"Be strong to bear, O heart!
   Nothing is vain;
Strive not, for life is care,
   And God sends pain;
Heaven is above, and there
   Rest will remain!

"Be strong to love, O heart!
   Love knows not wrong;
Didst thou love creatures even,
   Life were not long;
Didst thou love God in heaven,
   Thou wouldst be strong."

VII.
CHRIST'S MISSION TO DEAF EARS.

Isaiah xxxv. 5.

THE character portrayed as representing the Christian in the prophecies, as well as in the words of Christ, represents a wide-awake, alert, hopeful, enthusiastic, aggressive personality. It is gracious and gentle and loving, but all of these incarnated in a strong and earnest life. Christ's idea of a Christian is set forth with great clearness in the twelfth chapter of Luke, where he says to his disciples, indicating their attitude after he should be gone: "Let your loins be girded about, and your lights burning; and ye yourselves like unto men that wait for their Lord." Again and again he cautions them against drowsiness of soul and the danger of being asleep on guard when the Master shall come. We need to be frequently reminded of the danger of falling into a careless attitude concerning our duty and the responsibilities and privileges that belong to us. Nothing is more important to us in our Christian career than that our ears shall be open to hear the voices which speak to us of duty and of opportunity.

There are many ways by which men and women are made deaf to the higher calls upon them. Sometimes the ear is closed through a sluggish content. There is such a thing as pharisaical self-complacency, a settling down at ease and being satisfied with what we have already accomplished. To do that is to cease to grow and to cease all earnestness of effort in the higher culture of our own nature for the conquest of our fellow men for Christ. There are many warnings in the Scripture against this condition, and a "wo" is declared upon those that are "at ease in Zion." Contentment in its true sense is, of course, desirable and right. Paul said: "I have learned, in whatsoever state I am, therewith to be content." We are assured again that "godliness with contentment is great gain." But there is a sort of contentment which is not an accompaniment of godliness. It is a contentment that is born of laziness, of a willingness to do nothing and accomplish nothing. There is a discontent which is selfish and which is born of a spirit of rebellion against God; that is wicked. But there is a discontent that is holy and divine. The proper attitude of the earnest Christian is that of the listener with open ear, open mind, open heart, longing to know more of God, hungering and thirsting for his righteousness, alert to receive indications of his will, and with every enlargement of soul trying to do service for the Master. As Dr. Barrows, of Boston, says, it is not the selfish, grasping heart which is unsatisfied; it is the loving and generous one. The baby born with such a nature makes friends with all the world. As a child, it claims the whole school as playmates. Arriving at maturity, there is still the eager outstretching for more to love. The happy mother rejoices in the wider opportunity for the tendrils of affection to clasp and cling. She watches her little ones grow to manhood and womanhood, and rejoices in grandchildren on whom to pour out the rich balm of her heart. There is a vast difference between the unsatisfied heart—unsatisfied because conscious of latent powers that are God-given and hungry for development—and the dissatisfied heart. The unsatisfied heart is alert for every good that comes, and full of gratitude in response. But the dissatisfied heart frets and fumes because its selfish achievements do not bring it peace. The man or woman with the open mind and heart may see dear one after dear one pass away; yet there is ever an onreaching of affection which holds like a magnet all who come within its influence. One might speak of the sun as unsatisfied in the same sense. In these March days it is calling after the buried roots and seeds, and slowly but surely awakening the spring-time. Afterward it will gently lure on the forests and fields toward the summer, and still later bring about the golden wealth of the autumn harvest. It is ever calling on and upward. It is so with the unsatisfied soul. It sees ever in perspective joy and love, and stretches out its wings to meet them. The immortal life is to it an unquestioned reality. How else could the instinctive longings of the heart be gratified? When there are in a community enough such souls to leaven it, the tone of that place is optimistic. If things are not right, they will be made so. There is no halting-place for the unsatisfied heart. It springs from better to better, finding satisfaction only in the infinite Life and Love.

Sometimes our ears are closed through recklessness. No one can estimate the sorrows and defeats that come to our human life through the ear that is stopped up because of indifference. We are pursuing many things that now seem good to us, when, if we had an open mind to hear the warnings of history and divine truth, we should know that we would be much worse off than we are if we were to succeed in our pursuit.

But it is not only ourselves that we destroy because of deafness brought on by our recklessness and indifference. Down in the fire-room of a big steamer that was lying at the wharf in New York, a young man was told to do a certain piece of work in connection with the pumps. There were two pumps close together in the room—one for feeding the boiler and the other to use in case the ship should take fire. This latter one was capable of throwing a volume of water as large as a man's body. The young man, who had been employed on the ship for three years, and who, when he concentrated his attention on it, knew all that was necessary concerning the work in hand, went to the wrong pump and removed the cap from the fire-pump. In a moment he discovered his error, but the force of the water was so great that he could not replace the cap on the pump. Without a word he ran to the deck, left the steamer, and took the cars for his home in another State. Before the accident was discovered the water had filled the hold of the vessel, and in spite of every effort the vessel sank, and many thousands of dollars of damage was done. What do you suppose was this young man's answer to the question as to the cause of the accident? It was in four little words, "I did not think." How much sorrow we are giving other people through ignorance which is our own fault, and which would be dispelled in a moment were we to open our ears to the words of knowledge sounding within our hearing.

VIII.
THE SOLDIER'S HOME-COMING.

Isaiah xxxv. 10.

THE people and the newspapers have all been talking this week about the home-coming of the soldiers. The bells have rung, the whistles have blown, the streets have been filled with welcoming crowds, banquets have been spread, and everything we have known how to do we have been doing to welcome back the volunteers who went away a few months ago as our substitutes, to sustain the national honor and do the duty which the people felt was rightfully laid upon our government to do.

These young men know much more about a soldier's life than they did when they went away. Much of the glamour of it has disappeared. The hardship of the march, the discipline of the daily drill whether one feels like it or not, the restraints of military discipline, the monotony of a soldier's fare, the hard side of a soldier's cot, the loneliness of a camp far distant from home, the realization that "hope deferred maketh the heart sick"—all these remained after the glamour had disappeared.

But now that it is over and they come home to be mustered out, how soon all these things will be forgotten. The welcoming cheers, the faces of those they love, the luxuries of home made doubly attractive by months of hardship, will soon dispel the memory of the trials of the past, and even those hardships will receive an enchantment as the retreating sun throws its glow upon them in the distance. Who cares for the homesickness when he is home again? Who cares for the loneliness when he strikes glad hands and looks into happy eyes? Who cares for the hunger in the presence of the banquet? It is hard to remember yesterday's hunger when we are full to-day.

I have seized on these thoughts not to talk about the Spanish war, but to talk about the greater war in which we are all enlisted and which we must carry forward until death musters us out. I think it is a good thing for us to think of life as a battle and to count ourselves the soldiers of Jesus Christ. If we have that thought in our mind it will help us to submit our wills to the will of our Leader. The first thing a soldier has to learn is how to obey. He must submit his will absolutely to the authority of those who are over him. He may often think that mistakes are being made; he may be sure that somebody has blundered; but his place is to go straight on and do the thing he is ordered to do. As soldiers of Jesus we can rest assured that our Captain will never blunder. There is due from us a perfect and complete obedience to our Lord.

The true soldier never asks the question whether the service which he is called upon to perform is one of high dignity or not. It is for him to obey and do faithfully the duty at hand. Such Christian soldiers are always a godsend to the church. Henry Ward Beecher was once about to take a ride behind a horse which he had hired from a livery stable. He regarded the horse admiringly, and remarked: "That is a fine-looking animal. Is he as good as he looks?" The owner replied: "Mr. Beecher, that horse will work in any place you put him, and do all that any horse can do." The preacher eyed the horse still more admiringly, and then remarked: "I wish to goodness he was a member of my church!"

To be ready with military promptness, to seize hold of present duty whether it seem great or small, is to make ourselves helpful allies of Jesus Christ. Dr. Guthrie, the great Scotch preacher, relates that he was once stopping at Inverary Castle as the guest of the Duke of Argyle. A great many distinguished guests were present, among whom was Mr. Gladstone, who was premier at the time. Morning and evening worship was held in the chapel. It was the habit of one of the Duke's daughters to play the little organ, and they sang the Psalms, and Dr. Guthrie read the Scriptures and exhorted every morning. Among the most constant of his hearers, and close to his side every morning, was Mr. Gladstone, and Dr. Guthrie said that the intense earnestness with which he listened was an inspiration. One morning the organist was not in her place and there was no one to play the tune. Dr. Guthrie looked around upon the assemblage, and invited some one to come forward and play the organ, but they were all timid and did not start. "Oh, I wish I had a precentor if I can not get an organist!" said Dr. Guthrie. And with that he heard a voice by his side, saying: "Permit me, doctor." He looked up, and there was the great, tall form of Gladstone, who had taken the psalm-book in his hand, and all the congregation rose, while to the grand old tune of "Martyrdom" Gladstone led the morning Psalm,—

"Be merciful to me, O God; thy mercy unto me
Do thou extend, because my soul doth put her trust in thee."

There was a pathos about his singing that made him, to his astonishment, find that he was singing almost a solo to the weeping accompaniment of many. As the premier of England, holding the helm of the great empire, in ringing tones sang that penitential cry to God, every one felt that it was true that he put his trust in him. That was done in the true spirit of the Christian soldier.

To think of ourselves as soldiers of Jesus Christ will bring us into a conscious brotherhood with all other Christians. There is nothing like sharing the hardships and dangers of a soldier's life to break down all prejudice and caste. One of the Rough Riders, himself one of the wealthy volunteers from the fashionable wing of New York society, said that the whitest men in the fight at Santiago were the black men. The black cavalrymen were the first to carry away the wounded of the Rough Riders, and by their cheerfulness and brave assistance saved many lives. They so won the admiration and respect of their fellow soldiers that all thought of prejudice against them because of their color disappeared. One night a band of the colored soldiers came over to serenade Colonels Wood and Roosevelt, and when Colonel Roosevelt made a little speech, thanking them for their songs, one big black sergeant got up and said: "It's all right, colonel; we'se all Rough Riders now."

A colored soldier speaks with the same sort of appreciation from their standpoint. He says:

"In the charge up San Juan hill a ball entered my cheek. The artery was cut and was spurting blood. I managed to get back of the firing-line somehow, but the doctor said he could do nothing for me. Just then a Rough Rider came up. He put his thumb on my jugular vein and held it there two hours. Two hours—and me a negro! He saved my life!"

IX.
HOW TO GET EVERYTHING YOU WANT.

Psalm xxiii.

I NOTICED when I announced my theme, "How to Get Everything You Want," in the public congregation, that there was a good deal of smiling and shrewd looks at each other, as if you thought that I was talking outside of the record. But I certainly was keeping within the record. At least David, a man of large experience, thought so. He said, "The Lord is my shepherd, I shall not want." And again he says, "They that trust in the Lord shall not want any good thing."

Let us think over for a moment the things that normal, wholesome human nature wants. We want peace, rest of soul; but that is provided for us, for does not our Psalmist say—and every sincere Christian finds it true—"He maketh me to lie down in green pastures"? One of our great wants is a thirst of soul for that which satisfies the spirit and gives happiness, and that is provided for.

We are assured that "he leadeth me beside the still waters." A deceived heart which is led astray to seek its best good in this world, in sensual, earthly pleasures, "feedeth on ashes," but no honest Christian ever feeds on ashes. He has green pastures and quiet, cool waters that are abundant.

Another great want is for something to refresh us every now and then and stimulate us to a new impulse. Even the most resolute and self-sufficient natures are ofttimes weary and ready to faint, and need to have their enthusiasm and hopefulness restored. But that is all arranged for in God's plan. David says, "He restoreth my soul." We have just found out that in dealing with soldiers it is better to restore them and refresh them, than it is to try and make them tough by getting them used to a sickly climate. At the breaking out of the war with Spain it was thought best to send our volunteers down into a hot climate, full of malaria, and let them get used to what they would have to stand when they went to Cuba. This is just the reverse policy from what the English follow in India. The British Government prepares its armies for work in the hot lowlands of the East by sending them up into the mountains till they are thoroughly refreshed and toned up in their strength and vigor, and while they are still in this condition they are brought down for a short, decisive campaign. It is believed that this is the great secret of the victorious English army in the East. Our officers are finding that it is a good deal wiser than our own course. Our soldiers had the life and vitality cooked out of them by weeks of suffering in a depressing climate before they were sent forward to battle. The Lord, who never makes mistakes, works on the plan of refreshing his soldiers very often. He takes us up into the highlands of faith and hope and restores our souls.

Another longing of the soul is for a guide. There are many perplexing paths, and it is not always easy to know which path to take. Sometimes when we pray, our prayers do not seem to come in touch with God's heart. George Macdonald, the poet-novelist, one of the most reverent and spiritual Christians of our time, voices a frequent experience when he sings,—

> "My prayer-bird was cold,—would not away,
> Altho I set it on the edge of the nest.
> Then I bethought me of the story old,—
> Love-fact or loving fable, thou know'st best,—
> How, when the children had made sparrows of clay,
> Thou mad'st them birds, with wings to flutter and fold
> Take, Lord, my prayer in thy hand, and make it pray.

> "My poor clay-sparrow seems turned to a stone,
> And from my heart will neither fly nor run.
> I can not feel as thou and I both would;

> But, Father, I am willing,—make me good.
> What art thou, Father, for but to help thy son?
> Look deep, yet deeper, in my heart, and there,
> Beyond what I can feel, read thou the prayer."

And surely that is what God has promised to do. The promise is that the Holy Spirit shall help us in our infirmities; and the Psalmist says, "He leadeth me in the paths of righteousness for his name's sake."

But it is oftentimes a lonely world and we want company. We get homesick for sympathy. There are dark places to go through, times of sickness and pain and death, and we want somebody that can go with us all the way. And that, too, has not been forgotten, for does not David say: "Yea, tho I walk through the valley of the shadow of death, I will fear no evil, for thou art with me."

Dr. Cuyler, himself a blessed type of Christian triumph in old age, says that old age is too often represented under the dreary similitude of winter, with its bitter, biting winds whistling through leafless boughs, and its frozen clods ringing like iron beneath our feet. But there is a more genial season that bears the picturesque name of Indian summer, when nature puts on a sweet smile before the wintry frosts set in, and the lingering foliage is clad in crimson and gold. A Christian life has its bright Indian summer also. Graces adorn the veteran Christian and beautify him like the scarlet glories of the autumn forest; like shocks of corn ripened in sunshine and shower are the happy men and women who, tho they may be "eighty years young," still "bring forth fruit in old age" that is savory to the taste. And death is only a bright shadow to a man who has wrought with earnest heart, growing kindly and loving in spirit. It does not come to him with any pall of gloom. You have all watched a railroad train slowing up gently as it came into the station with its passengers. Never was there spoken a sweeter answer than that of the good Cardinal Manning to one who asked him how he was, to which he returned only this, "I am slowing gently into the station!"

But, some one says, "There are other things I want. I want to be comforted." Well, "Thy rod and thy staff, they comfort me." But another says, "I want more than comfort and sympathy and food, and quiet times; I want joy." Listen, "Thou anointest my head with oil." And if that is too figurative and Oriental for you, listen to the words of Jesus, "That my joy might remain in you, and that your joy might be full;" and again, "Your heart shall rejoice, and your joy no man taketh from you." Are you fearful, desiring an insurance policy that will last all the way through? Here it is—"Surely goodness and mercy shall follow me all the days of my life, and I will dwell in the house of the Lord forever."

And now for a cap-sheaf to go over the top. Out on the farms, when they shock up the grain they take one sheaf and open it so as to come down over the peak of the shock and make it turn rain. We have a cap-sheaf here that is warranted to cover everything that has been left out by any forgetfulness—"My cup runneth over." And that was not through any favoritism or accident on David's account. Christ lays it down as a general proposition that God always deals with us that way when we open our hearts to him and surrender ourselves to completely do his will. He says: "Judge not, and ye shall not be judged; condemn not and ye shall not be condemned: forgive and ye shall be forgiven: give and it shall be given unto you; good measure, pressed down, and shaken together, and running over shall men give into your bosom." And not only here will it run over, but our joy shall run over in heaven. Peter Mackenzie, a quaint Wesleyan preacher in England, was once preaching from the text, "And they sang a new song," and he said: "Yes, there will be singing in heaven, and when I get there I shall want to have David with his harp and Paul and Peter and other saints gather round for a song. And I will announce a hymn from the Wesleyan Hymnal,

'Let us sing hymn No. 749, "My God, my Father, while I stray."' But some one will say: 'That won't do. You are in heaven, Peter; there is no straying here.' And I will say: 'Yes, that is so. Let us sing No. 651, "Tho waves and storms go o'er my head."' But another saint will say, 'Peter, you are in heaven now; you forget that there are no storms here!' 'Well, I will try again. No. 536, "Into a world of ruffians sent."' 'Peter! Peter!' some one will say, 'we will put you out unless you stop giving out inappropriate hymns,' and I will ask, 'What shall we sing?' And they will say, 'Sing the new song, the song of Moses and the Lamb.'"

X.
THE SPIRITUAL FARMER.

Hosea x. 12 (Rev. Ver.).

THIS figure, which compares the soul of man to a field, is a very common one in the Scriptures. Christ uses it in more than one parable, but especially in that oft-quoted parable of the Sower, where the Son of man is represented as a sower who went forth to sow, and some of the seed which he scattered fell by the wayside on hearts and minds so trodden down by the hoof and wheel of worldly things that they had no power of absorbing it, and the seed was caught up and carried away by the wicked one. Some fell upon stony places where there was a little earth, but only a little, and here the seed immediately sprang up and for the moment was joyously appreciated, but there was so little soil and so little opportunity for root that when tribulation or persecution arose the new life which had promised so much withered away. Some fell among thorns, those hard and biting thorns of the cares of this world and the deceitfulness of riches, which choked out the heavenly seed, and tho it grew with promise in the rich soil, the thorns so occupied the ground and monopolized the affections and purpose of the soul that no harvest was returned. But other seed fell on good ground, into the minds and hearts of men who heard it with reverence and gave it such understanding thoughts that it grew and flourished so that it brought forth in some cases thirty, in some sixty, and in still others an hundredfold.

In still another parable the Savior sets forth the human mind and heart as a field where rival sowers are competing for an opportunity to sow their seed and win a harvest. Here the Son of man sows the good seed and afterward the devil comes as an enemy and sows tares in the field; and in many cases the loving purpose of the Son of man is defeated and the harvest yields only bundles of tares unworthy of a place in the heavenly garner and fit only for destruction.

Paul in his first letter to the Corinthians uses the same figure when he says, "Ye are God's husbandry," or, as the marginal rendering has it, "God's tilled land." In each of these places the figure is used to represent the human heart as comparatively submissive, receiving simply the tilling of the divine Husbandman. That is one side of the truth. But all the truth is not obtained from that side. Truth is many-sided, and we must look at it on all sides in order to get a comprehensive view. The Scripture to which I call your attention uses this same figure, but looks at it from another standpoint, and shows man to be at once the field and the farmer in his own inner nature. The prophet Hosea calls upon his people to plow their own hearts, and sow the field themselves, in expectation of reaping through the divine mercy and grace. It is from that standpoint that I wish to study it with you at this time.

The text is not addressed to those who have not known anything of God; not to the heathen who are in utter darkness about spiritual things, but to those who have known the Lord, whose spiritual nature has in the past had more or less cultivation, but who through lack of watchfulness, or from other causes, have failed to do their duty, and the heart field has become hardened and unproductive. Any one accustomed to the terminology of the farm knows what fallow ground means. The soil was once in cultivation and yielded crops, but through indolence or absorption in other matters the farmer has let his plows stand idle in the springtime and the ground has become packed and hard. Weeds and thorns have again taken possession of the soil. Such a field must have thorough work. It will take a strong team, and a staunch plow with a sharp point and a bright glare, to cut down deep and turn the soil upside down, exposing the roots of wild growth that have taken possession. The prophet Hosea says those who have become cold and indifferent in their relations to God are in that condition. And he calls upon all such to break up the fallow ground.

The question naturally arises, How can we plow up the fallow ground of our own hearts? The first great force of spiritual cultivation is prayer. And I do not mean a single outpouring of the soul to God under some sudden impulse of trying need which drives us to the throne of grace for the shelter and protection we have been indifferent about on ordinary occasions; but I wish to urge the great truth that definite, purposed, regular prayer to God, at a stated time, because a man's judgment indicates to him the wisdom of it, because his conscience impels him to the duty, because his heart yearns for the divine communion, is the mightiest force known to mankind for keeping the soul in well-ordered spiritual cultivation. I do not mean to say that it is not right to go to God in cases of special necessity when we are threatened with utter shipwreck and have come to the end of our own strength. It is the marvel of God that he will and does hear us when we thus come to him in faith. But I wish to put the emphasis upon the duty and privilege of the children of God to keep their hearts reverent, worshipful, and in a proper state of cultivation to receive every good seed the Divine Sower may seek to plant in the soul, and in a proper condition to bring to rapid harvest the graces of the Spirit. I feel compelled to urge this message upon you, because I fear that the habit of stated prayer at regular times is to some extent falling into neglect. And I am sure that no Christian can live as he ought to live, enjoy the heavenly communion as his privilege, exercise the influence that he ought over his fellows, and yield constant glory to God, without conscientiously devoting certain time every day to sincere worship of God. Prayer develops a spiritual atmosphere in the mind and heart of him who prays, in which it is easy for the spiritual life to grow and thrive.

There is an interesting article in one of our leading magazines of a recent issue, in which the writer discusses what he calls "art atmosphere." He says that America has no atmosphere that helps to stimulate artistic production and keep alive the glow of artistic sympathy. He adds that many an artist has come home from the great art centers of Europe after years of quiet fervor and wholesome growth, only to find his ardor checked, and to feel his talent wither and grow feeble or misshapen. Proceeding to discuss the remedy for this, the writer declares that, after all, the matter mainly rests with the artists themselves. The atmosphere will come when they begin to make it— as grown trees provide the shelter in which younger trees grow up and flourish—by striking root in the American soil, by living in sound artistic sympathy with things around them and with the community where they have made their home.

So there are people who have intellectual conceptions concerning spiritual things which are highly creditable, and who are thoroughly Christian in theory. But the atmosphere of their hearts, if not entirely un-Christian, is entirely non-Christian. It is the divine influence of prayer that creates an atmosphere in which Christian truth flourishes. He would be a very unwise farmer who would never get his plows to work in the field until the last bushel of wheat had gone from the granary, and the last ear of corn from the crib, and he was driven into the field by the lashing of his hunger; yet the people who never pray except when they get into trouble, or are driven to extremity, will find themselves illustrated by such a figure. The wise farmer plows his fields at the regular time without reference to the amount of corn on hand. He turns the soil over and over again, that he may keep it in a proper state of cultivation to grow whatever seed he may design for it. So these sensitive fields of the heart need the constant culture that comes from consciously opening the heart to God and communing with him concerning all the deep longings and aspirations of our highest nature.

XI.
CHRIST'S KINGDOM OF CHARACTER.

Romans xiv. 17-18.

THIS chapter and the one following contain a remarkably interesting discussion of the Christian's privilege and duty of denying himself in small matters, in order to the comfort or upbuilding of a weaker brother. It is an appeal for broad-minded, large-hearted, well-grounded, Christian character. Paul urges that if one has been won to the slightest confidence in Christ it is our duty to receive him into the fellowship of Christians, even tho his faith is weak, and his knowledge of Christ far from satisfying. And he urges that this weak brother should not be received to a debating-school of doubtful disputes about insignificant things, and things that are non-essential to the building up of a noble and Christlike manhood. Paul presses home upon the people to whom he is writing the importance of the graces of Christian charity and forbearance. He declares that it is not wise or profitable to argue with a man and dispute with him as to whether he shall eat all kinds of food or confine himself to herbs only. Neither is it worth while haggling with another about particular holy days. It is better, he says, to let each one follow his own conscience. If, however, we find that our indulgence in certain things that are in dispute causes offense to those who are weak in the faith, and they are likely to be turned out of the way by our conduct, Paul argues that the spirit of Christ will lead us in such a case to deny ourselves, not on any basis of abstract right, but in the Christ spirit of self-denial, in order to bear the burdens of the weak, to strengthen "the bruised reed," and protect "the smoking flax." The gist of Paul's argument is this, that what we eat or drink, or what particular ceremonies we keep or do not keep, are such small and insignificant matters compared to the great end of our Christian life, the development of the graces of the Spirit and the building up of a noble and holy character, that it is exceedingly unwise to quarrel about them or to lose time in discussing them; and, above all, is it foolish to run the risk of seriously hurting any soul and turning any trembling footstep out of the way of right by our stubbornness concerning such things. "For," says the great preacher, "the kingdom of God is not meat and drink; but righteousness and peace and joy in the Holy Ghost. For he that in these things serveth Christ is acceptable to God and approved of men."

Let us examine these constituent elements which enter into the life blood of a Christian character. Righteousness stands at the head of the list. One is reminded by this declaration of Paul of that poetic and beautiful discourse of Christ in which he urges upon his disciples that they should not be anxious about worldly necessities. "Take no thought for your life," he says, "what ye shall eat, or what ye shall drink; nor yet for your body, what ye shall put on. Is not the life more than meat, and the body than raiment? Behold the fowls of the air: for they sow not, neither do they reap, nor gather into barns; yet your heavenly Father feedeth them. Are ye not much better than they? Which of you by taking thought can add one cubit unto his stature? And why take ye thought for raiment? Consider the lilies of the field, how they grow; they toil not, neither do they spin: and yet I say unto you, that even Solomon in all his glory was not arrayed like one of these. Wherefore, if God so clothe the grass of the field, which to-day is, and to-morrow is cast into the oven, shall he not much more clothe you, O ye of little faith? Therefore take no thought, saying, What shall we eat? or, What shall we drink? or,

Wherewithal shall we be clothed? . . . for your heavenly Father knoweth that ye have need of all these things. But seek ye first the kingdom of God, and his righteousness; and all these things shall be added unto you." This beautiful paragraph illustrates the emphasis which Jesus Christ everywhere puts upon righteousness.

Naturally peace follows righteousness. If we are right toward God we have peace with God. A doctor who was visiting a Christian patient had himself long been anxious to feel that he was at peace with God. The Spirit had convinced him of his sin and need, and he longed to possess that peace which the world can not give. On one occasion, addressing himself to the sick man, he said: "I want you to tell me just what it is—this believing and getting happiness, faith in Jesus, and all that sort of thing which brings peace." His patient replied: "Doctor, I have felt in regard to my health that I could do nothing, and I have put my case in your hands; I am trusting to you. That is exactly what every poor sinner must do in the Lord Jesus." This reply greatly awakened the doctor's surprise, and a new light broke into his soul. "Is that all?" he exclaimed; "simply trusting in the Lord Jesus? I see it as I never did before. He has done the work: yes, Jesus said on the cross, 'It is finished,' and at another time,

'Whosoever believeth in Him shall not perish, but hath everlasting life.'" From the sick-bed the doctor went, a happy man, rejoicing that his sins were washed away in the blood of the Lamb.

Righteousness and peace naturally bring joy, being the normal soil out of which joy may grow. Obedience to Christ, righteousness which keeps his commandments, and peace born of confidence in God, are open windows through which heaven's sunshine floods the heart and makes it sing for joy. Joy can not be produced by command by outside conditions. It cannot be bought with gold, nor be bestowed at will. True joy is born of the condition of the soul. But you will notice that this is joy of a peculiar kind. It is "joy in the Holy Ghost." That is, joy in the consciousness of living in the presence of God. If we are sinning against God, then the consciousness that God sees us, that his eye beholds our conduct, and that he is near us, is a source of terror; but if we are at peace with him, then the consciousness of his presence is a comfort and joy to us.

A great deal of attention has recently been attracted to what is known as the "X-ray," a discovery by which Professor Roentgen has photographed through the human hand and revealed upon a photographic plate the skeleton within. There are already many reports of the success of scientists in using the X-ray to discover fractures in the human skeleton, and derangements of the internal organs by aid of the "new light." While at the first thought the idea of having one's form photographed so that the inner mystery of the skeleton may be seen by human eyes seems to shock one, yet it is easy to understand the gladness with which a patient might submit to such an examination under the direction of the physician in whom he had confidence, knowing that the better knowledge thus acquired would give added probability of recovery. So, to the soul that trusts in God, the consciousness of the presence of the Holy Spirit dwelling with us, knowing all about us, seeing our inmost heart, causes joy; for we know that it is the eye not of a detective or a critic, but the eye of the Great Physician, the eye of Infinite Love, that beholds imperfections only to heal them. The confidence that God means always best for us can not but be a constant source of joy.

A small boy was at a table where his mother was not near to take care of him, and a lady next to him volunteered her services. "Let me cut your steak for you," she said; "if I can cut it the way you like it," she added, with some degree of doubt. "Thank you," the boy responded, accepting her courtesy, "I shall like it the way you cut it, even if you do not cut it the way I like it." Any mother would be proud to have a boy as polite as that. And if it sprang from a genuine inner content and courtesy of the soul, it was the foundation of a joyous life. That illustrates the true spirit and source of Christian joy. God will give us what is best. Having given us the Lord Jesus Christ, he will freely, with him, give us all things. With this confidence and assurance it is possible for the Christian to look up into the face of God and say in regard to the daily portion of his life, in the language of the little boy, "I shall like it the way you cut it, even if you do not cut it the way I like it."

XII.
RELIGIOUS GADDERS.

Jeremiah ii. 36.

THE Lord, speaking to his church in the days of Jeremiah, makes this very pertinent inquiry, "Why gaddest thou about so much to change thy way? Thou also shalt be ashamed of Egypt, as thou wast ashamed of Assyria." That is, they would take up with a new thing for awhile, and have all the enthusiasm of a new convert, but having no settled and fixed purpose of devotion, they would stray off again after the next new sensation that came along. The result of all this was that they had no permanent place of comfort and found no rest unto their souls.

This tribe of religious gadders are not without multitudes of representatives in our time. They go about hearing the last new preacher or the last experiment in church choirs, or to see something new in architecture, until they know the rounds of the churches better than anybody else in town. They can taste more sermons and get less good out of them than any one in the city. They get to be practically religious vagrants, who go tramping about getting lodging for a sermon or a service here and there, but neither doing nor receiving good.

The Psalmist says that it is those who are planted in the house of the Lord who are flourishing and fruitful. If you were to plant out a young apple-tree in the spring, and take it up and plant it in some place else every week, it wouldn't be long until it would be too dead to sprout anywhere. A great many people are that way in their religious life. Many of them have their name on the church record at some one church, and are seen there on great occasions, but for the most of the time they go gadding about after every new sensation. Such people are not really planted in God's house, and they are always shrunken and shriveled and dried up at the roots, spiritually. I never knew one single man or woman of that sort who had any real spiritual influence anywhere.

In the book of Revelation the Savior declares that it is his purpose to make those who are conquerors in his name pillars in the house of the Lord. A pillar is a very stable sort of a thing; it does not gad about the church or to different churches. There is as much difference between a person who establishes himself in the church, and in the work of the church, so that he is always on hand Sunday morning and Sunday night, and at prayer-meeting, and at any revival service that may be held—who can always be counted on and relied upon to do his part—and people who give their names to the church and then go gadding about from one place to another, so that the pastor never can tell whether they will be present or not, as there is between a church pillar which is a part of the very church itself, and a vagrant fly that wanders in through the window and crawls for an hour now and then on the ceiling or in the pew. Religious gadders are never of any service to a church. They do not stay long enough in any one place. Church life is a growth. A church is like the human body: it has head, and heart, and digestive apparatus, and muscles, and hands, and feet. It is all the time taking in people, and, if it can, digesting them into the strength of its working force. But a great many people remain on its hands undigested. They are not digestible; they do not give themselves up reverently and earnestly to the work of the Lord. Therefore they get no real good out of the church; they give no part of their real personality to the church, and because of that the church has no opportunity to be of any great comfort or blessing to them.

There is an old phrase, "belonging to the church," which means a great deal if used in its full sense. To give one's self up to the church so that a spiritual home is found there, a spiritual garden in which to grow and blossom for God and humanity, is a great thing; but to call it belonging to the church when the church is only used as a club-room where one goes in occasionally and takes a dish of ice cream, or a meal, is a religious farce. Life is very short at best, and we should gad about as little as possible. To do our best work we must run our religious roots down into some definite church home and put the full force of our strength into the work in that place. In that way we come to count for something. Somebody relies on us, we are able to carry some burdens for others, and that consciousness is a constant source of comfort. As the years pass over us in our church home our branches of influence spread, and we become a source of comfort and strength to many who are newer in the church work than ourselves. It is only in this way that the psalmist's promise shall come true, that the righteous shall be fat and flourishing even to the last, and bear fruit in old age. If you want to come to be an old man or an old woman not as a withered and dying bough thrown out in the street as useless, but as a great wide-spreading tree about whom the loving interest of younger men and women clusters, then you must forswear gadding, and establish yourself as one of the reliable factors of church life.

XIII.
HOW TO BECOME MORE TRULY RELIGIOUS.

Eph. vi.

PAUL did not for a moment accept the mediæval idea of what it takes to constitute a religious life. In his view spirituality was not something unnatural, which required one to withdraw from the ordinary pleasures and labors of a healthy human life. In order to be religious Paul did not understand that a man must cease to deal earnestly with the actual toil and social relations of the world. Children were to show their religion in the proper respect and reverence which they gave to their parents. Parents were to show the true religious spirit of their lives by the kindness and considerate thoughtfulness with which they dealt with their children. Employees were to show the sincerity and genuineness of their religious faith by the straightforward honesty of their work. They were to regard their work as not done for their employer only, but with reference to Christ, doing it "not with eye-service, as men-pleasers; but as the servants of Christ, doing the will of God from the heart; with good-will doing service, as to the Lord, and not to men: knowing that whatsoever good thing any man doeth, the same shall he receive of the Lord, whether he be bond or free." The religion of employers is also clearly stated. It is to be revealed in the just and thoughtful consideration with which they deal with those who labor for them. According to Paul the truly religious employer will have his life largely influenced by the consciousness that he himself is only an employee in the vineyard of the Lord, and will treat his employees in the same spirit with which he desires to be treated by the Divine Husbandman.

Paul then sets forth the condition upon which such a religious life can be maintained. First of all, there must be intelligence in the armor of the soul. A man must stand firm because he is thoroughly entrenched in an intelligent faith in God. His loins must be girt about with truth. The whole nature must be held together by that strong girdle of truth. And how soon a man begins to go to pieces when inflexible truth ceases to be a characteristic of his manhood! Truth is the girdle of the religious life. Cut that girdle and the strength soon goes. Then there must be the breastplate of righteousness. Davy Crockett's old proverb, "Be sure you're right, and then go ahead," is founded upon this rock of eternal truth. A man dares to go ahead when he is sure he is right. If we wear the breastplate of righteousness we can advance facing any foe. The shoes of peace go on easily and fit well when the breastplate of righteousness and the girdle of truth have already been tested. The shield of faith comes naturally in such a combination. Faith has its natural source in truth and righteousness. You can make a shield out of such faith to quench every fiery dart of the wicked one. The helmet of salvation comes easily to the head of the man whose heart is right, whose life is truthful, whose arm wears the shield of faith and whose feet walk in shoes of peace.

Such a character is prepared to wield the sword of the Spirit, which is the Word of God. The Bible, while it helps to put on an armor like this, is also, on the other hand, only thoroughly understood and worthily used by the soul thus armored. There are passages that only the righteous man can understand; there are deeps that couch beneath in God's Word, where only truthful eyes can see into the depths; there are clouds full of mercy, where the eyes of faith alone can peer; there are valleys full of the hush of the Spirit, where only feet moccasined with the gospel of peace can ever tread. There are mysteries where the proudest intellect is blind unless the head be clothed upon with the helmet of salvation.

But a sword was made for service, and the religious life is a life of service. True spirituality is developed by earnest, helpful service of the Lord. It is positive, not negative. It is not the sleep of the spirit, nor the death of the spirit, but the life of the spirit. The spiritual man is a worker; he is buoyed up in his toil by visions that he catches through the eye of faith. He is strengthened against weariness by the consciousness that he is right. His fellowship with Jesus Christ gives him joy and courage.

Such a life of character and service is not only constantly fed, but will continually express itself in worship. Hence Paul says, "Praying always with all prayer and supplication in the Spirit, and watching thereunto with all perseverance and supplication for all saints."

These, then, are the great elements of a spiritual life—worship, service, intelligent attitude toward God and man, all resulting in character. All these characteristics act on each other. The Bible inspires devotion; worship inspires love for the Bible; both incite to helpfulness and service, while all result in character on the Christian plan. A well-rounded religious life according to the Christian idea must be the order and development of life with these characteristics. It is a whole-souled, healthy life in body, mind, and spirit. The most truly religious man ought to get the most joy out of all the senses. His taste for a good dinner, his sense of enjoyment in the flowers, his delight in social fellowship, his joy in the mere sense of being alive, ought to be all the keener because he stands out in the bright sunlight of God's day, in the humble but happy assurance that the girdle of truth is about his loins, the helmet of salvation is on his head, the shield of faith is between him and the enemy, and that his feet walk in ways of peace.

XIV.

THE WORSHIP OF THE HEART.

Acts xvii. 22-31.

PAUL was a plain talker. He had a great habit of preaching directly to the people the message he thought they personally ought to have. He had been walking about this city of Athens looking at the temples and observing the worship of the idols. Everywhere he saw heaps of offerings laid before these dumb and useless gods to propitiate them. Among them all he found this one altar erected to The Unknown God. This gave him a great opportunity. He found in it a good text and an easy way to bring to them his sublime message concerning the one God in whom all men live.

Naturally his message brings out in strong contrast true spiritual worship as against the formal offerings made to idols. He calls their attention to the fact that the piles of fruits and flowers and sacrifices laid before their idols would seem to indicate that their gods were poor and needed something that their worshipers could do for them;

but assures them that the one true God who made heaven and earth is not so poverty-stricken that he needs any kind of worship that men can offer with their hands.

And yet God longs for our worship. Why so, if he does not need it? That is our theme. God desires our worship not because he needs it, but because he has a Father's heart towards us and our love is as the affection of childhood to a great-hearted parent. While God does not need our worship, his heart desires it with an infinite desire. We want a great many things that we do not need, and appreciate them a great deal more than the things we need. It is the difference between receiving alms and receiving love. You do not need the box of roses that your best friend sent you on your birthday; you could have bought flowers for yourself; but there is something about the flowers your friend sends that no money could buy in any market. It is the kindly remembrance, the loving sympathy, the fellowship of souls, the fragrance of which is sweeter than any rose, that enters into your appreciation of such things. The worship of God is like that. It is not that God is a beggar and needs what we can lay on the altar before him, but that his great sensitive nature rejoices in the loving worship of his children. The psalmist understood it when he said: "Sacrifice and offering thou didst not desire: mine ears hast thou opened: burnt offering and sin offering hast thou not required. Then said I, Lo, I come; in the volume of the book it is written of me, I delight to do thy will, O my God: yea, thy law is within my heart." It is that heart worship and service that is dear to the heart of God. Psalm 40-6.

Of course if our hearts are full of love to God, our hands, too, will be kept busy serving him whom the soul loveth. You may always doubt the depth of your devotion when it expends itself in acclamations of praise and does not seek to do substantial service. An Irishman who had a very ragged coat was asked of what stuff it was made. "Faith, I don't know!" said he, "but I think the most of it is made of fresh air." The robe of some people's worship seems to be as ragged as that—it is mostly of fresh air. On the other hand, we must beware of reducing our worship to a dry formality. Dr. W. L. Watkinson, commenting on the passage, "Open thy mouth wide and I will fill it," says that some people clench their teeth, and if they are to be fed with truth at all, they have to be fed through their clenched teeth. That is not the true attitude. Hogarth, in painting Jupiter in the golden shower, introduces an old woman into the corner of the picture, trying one of the coins with her teeth. The people who try the promises of God in their teeth are not the people who are likely to see many visions.

The joyous and joy-giving member of the family circle is the one whose overflowing love goes out to all the family and whose heart is just as open to appreciate and receive love in return. It is so in the family of God. We must make the worship of God the great thing and the first thing in life, if our service is to be delightful to our Heavenly Father. We must beware of worldliness which may fill our atmosphere like a smoke until we have no spiritual perception. Balaam's ass saw the angel before his master did, and I don't doubt that many a horse or mule has as much spiritual perception as his owner, tho he be a church member. It was said of some of old that they were "sensual, not having the Spirit." Let us beware of that.

How clearly the difference between formality and sincerity in worship stands out in the story of the dinner in the house of the critical Simon, the Pharisee, where the woman came to Christ and washed his feet with her tears and wiped them with the hairs of her head. Jesus perceiving that the pharisaical Simon was trying him in his teeth, like Hogarth's woman in the picture, said to him: "Simon, I have somewhat to say unto thee. And he saith, Master, say on. There was a certain creditor which had two debtors: the one owed five hundred pence, and the other fifty. And when they had nothing to pay, he frankly forgave them both. Tell me, therefore, which of them will love him most? Simon answered and said, I suppose that he to whom he forgave most. And he said unto him, Thou hast rightly judged. And he turned to the woman and said unto Simon, Seest thou this woman? I entered into thine house, thou gavest me no water for my feet: but she hath washed my feet with tears, and wiped them with the hairs of her head. Thou gavest me no kiss: but this woman since the time I came in hath not ceased to kiss my feet. My head with oil thou didst not anoint: but this woman hath anointed my feet with ointment. Wherefore I say unto thee, Her sins, which are many, are forgiven; for she loved much." Sympathy and caresses and service are the natural offerings of love to the object of its devotion. It is a delight to render them to God when our hearts are overflowing with gratitude.

XV.

THE KIND OF HOLINESS PLEASING TO GOD.

John viii. 29.

THIS, it seems to me, is the supreme claim which Jesus Christ made for himself. No higher claim than this could be made. To say that the life of a man is always, under all circumstances, in sickness and in health, in prosperity and adversity, in youth and manhood, pleasing to God, entirely satisfactory to Him who created him and who knows perfectly the capacity of every function of human life, is the highest claim that could possibly be made for any one.

Christ is our model. At the very foundation of everything we can say about Christianity, we must agreee on this, that Jesus Christ himself was the first Christian, and that to be a Christian now is to follow after him and live our lives in his spirit.

It is idle for us to undertake to do the same things, in detail, that Jesus did. We can not all go and live in Palestine and be surrounded by the same circumstances of daily life that he knew.

But the marvelous triumphs of Christianity in the world, and the transformation it has wrought on civilization in whole races of people, show that the spirit of Christ may be communicated, and may be re-incarnated in living men and women from age to age. The supreme fact, then, of Christianity is that Christ's disciples are now, nearly nineteen hundred years after his ascension from the earth, to live the Christ-life here amid the conditions and circumstances of our modern time.

Christ could not have been the perfect Savior of men unless his life had been thus pleasing to God. And we cannot be perfect Christians unless we imitate the life of Jesus in this respect. There is, therefore, no more heart-searching question than this which I have selected from our theme, "Does my life please God?" The question is not whether I have clear perceptions, intellectually, of divine truth, or whether I have hours of spiritual vision when I long for the noblest and holiest things; but whether my life, the actual deeds which I perform from day to day, the conversations in which I indulge, the purposes which I form and seek to carry out, are such as commend themselves to Him who created me, who knows my life perfectly, who knows what I am capable of doing, and knows also what is for my highest interests.

Happily, we need not be in the dark concerning

what will please God, for Christ's life was pleasing to him, and that life is open to our study. We have only to put ourselves alongside of the life of Christ in its spirit and purpose and conduct to find out if we are living the same kind of a life. We must keep in mind always in this comparison between our life and that of Christ that it is not a question of quantity, but of quality. A little sparrow can live the life of a bird, using its wings to soar in the sky, as truly as an eagle. The quantity of its life is not equal, but in the quality it is of the same sort. We can not open the eyes of the blind, or unstop deaf ears, or recover lepers, or soothe fevers, or raise the dead, in the same way that Christ did; but we may live lives so fragrant with the same spirit of helpfulness and goodness and service that, while our lives are not as large as his, they shall be recognized both on earth and in heaven as of the same sort.

Judging from the life of Christ, we are sure that if our lives are to be pleasing to God they must be pure, holy lives. By that word "holy" I do not mean anything technical, and I do not utter the shibboleth of any faction. I think there has been no word in our time more abused, more frequently dragged in the mud of unwise strife, than that word "holiness." To be holy means to be healthy. To live a holy life means to be wholesome, healthy, and natural in our daily thinking and doing. Some people sneer at holiness as tho they thought a little sin added attractiveness and beauty to character. One might as well say that a little dirt improves drinking water; that a little chalk improves the quality of milk; that a little taint is good for meat; that a little treachery improves love, as to say that perfect holiness in character is not the most attractive and delightful thing that can characterize any human soul. The perfectly holy man will go about the work of life, dealing with his fellow men, in a perfectly natural, wholesome, and pure way. His conduct toward God and man will be perfectly sincere and open and genuine. If we turn from our lives to the life of Jesus we shall see that the holiness of Christ was just like that. There never was a man who lived a more simple, straightforward, natural life. He did not undertake to make himself holy by hiding himself away in quiet meditation, or by shutting himself off from troublesome and distracting relations with his fellow men. He went among people—the ordinary people, the common folks—of the towns and cities where he lived his life. He did not shun wicked people, or sick people, or beggars, or people who were in trouble. He met them one and all in an open, manly' way, and was in every case the good Neighbor, the helpful, true, honest, pure Man.

The Kind of Holiness Pleasing to God.

That is the sort of holiness we want now. It is the kind that is pleasing to God. In one of his beatitudes Jesus says: "Blessed are the pure in heart, for they shall see God"—not only in heaven, after awhile, but they shall see him here and now; see him in the strength of the mountains, see him in the dazzling glories of the midnight skies, see him in the beauty of the sunset, see him in the fragrance of the flowers, and above all, see him in the lives of men and women and in the onward progress of the coming victory of the kingdom of God on the earth.

Are our lives pleasing to God in this respect? Are they pure? Are we living wholesome lives? Are we keeping God's commandments? Are we living lives that in the clear sunshine of God's law can stand out as genuine? As our lives touch our fellow men are they kindly and benevolent and sincere? These are questions that ought to probe to the bottom of our hearts, for our lives cannot be healthy without that, and it is only a perfectly healthy, wholesome life that can please God.

XVI.
THE ANGELS PECULIAR TO SUMMER-TIME.

Amos viii. 1.

EVERY season has its peculiar blessings and its peculiar dangers. Our purpose is to study briefly the opportunities and privileges and blessings of summer-time that are likely to be angelic in their influence upon us.

The first angel of summer-time which suggests itself to the mind is that of beauty. It is the season of flowers and birds, and all the delightful coloring and fragrance and harmony of the physical world. It is a time of beauty. Beauty appeals to us in the greensward, in the foliage of the trees, in the flowers in the garden, in the birds coming back again from their winter exile, in the clouds balancing in the sky, in the changing lights and shadows on river and lake and sea—in all these, and in a thousand other ways, beauty appeals to us in summer.

The beautiful was intended to be an angel in its influence on our hearts. There is something

The Angels Peculiar to Summer-Time.

wrong with us when it does not have that effect. David said that God's gentleness made him great, and surely God shows us his gentleness in a wonderful way when he floods the world with beautiful colors and glorious harmonies these summer days. The beautiful things that meet us in the humblest door plat ought to soften our hearts to reverent gratitude, and awake in us the deep conviction that God is better to us by far than we deserve.

An Australian miner had reached the very last of his resources without finding a speck of gold, and there was nothing for him to do but to turn back on the morrow, while a mouthful of food was left, and retrace his steps as best he might to the nearest port. He flung down his tools in despair that last night, and staggered over the two or three miles of desert to the camp-fire. Next morning, early, after a great deal of sleep and very little food, he braced himself up to go back for his tools, knowing that they might bring the price of a meal or two when it came to the last. As he stumbled back that hot morning the way seemed very long, for his heart was too heavy to carry. At last he saw his wheelbarrow and pick standing upon the flat plain a little way off, and was wearily dragging on toward them, when he caught his toe against a stone deeply embedded in the sand, and fell down. This was the last straw that broke the camel's back. He lay there and cursed his luck bitterly, to think that he should nearly break his toe against the only stone in the whole district, after all his failure to find gold. He felt like a passionate child who kicks and breaks the thing which has hurt him, and he had to beat that stone before he could feel quiet. It was too firm in the sand for his hands to get it up; so in his rage he dug it up with his pick, intending to smash it; but it would not smash, for it was solid gold, and nearly as big as a baby's head. When he showed that great nugget of gold down at the seaport where he carried it, and told how bitter his heart was against God before he found it, he said with tears in his eyes, "Now, ma'am, I ask you, did I deserve this?"

Who is there of us coming out of the winter into the beauty and glory of springtime and summer, with all God's angels of beauty gathered about us, making the world a fairyland for us, who does not in thoughtful moments feel like saying, "Did I deserve this?" We know we did not; they are God's good angels come to us in pure mercy.

Another angel of summer-time is the angel of abundance. A generous God is our God. Summer-time is peculiarly the time of plenty. The poor do not need coal to keep them warm; work is abundant, food is abundant, and the whole world suns itself in the added ease and luxury of abundance. This is God's angel speaking to us of the heart of our Heavenly Father, who would make us know that there are riches for the soul, as well as for the body. The God who is prodigal with flowers and perfumes and rich colorings in the summer forests and skies, is not miserly with human souls. The writers of the Bible use in large measure the adjectives that tell of abundance when they speak of God's goodness in bestowing joy and glory upon his children. Especially is this true in the New Testament, after men have come to know the glory of God in the face of Jesus Christ. The words "abundant," "abundance," "riches of grace," "unsearchable riches," "abounding," "love beyond measure," and all such terms and phrases, that speak of unlimited generosity, are the common language of Paul's letters to those early Christian churches founded by him. This ought to be an angel to us. God means good to our souls; if they starve it is not his fault. "Blessed are they that do hunger and thirst after righteousness, for they shall be filled."

But childhood and old age are in great evidence in summer-time. They are often shut in in the winter, but the summer brings out both extremes. The baby carriages with their little angels of promise, and old age with its white crown of glory whom rheumatism has imprisoned in the chimney corner or by the furnace grate, now find their way into the crowd again. Both should be angels in their influence upon us. The sweet innocence of childhood, of which is "the kingdom of heaven," should recall to us the assurance of God's Word, that the Heavenly Father pitieth his children like a father and comforts them like a mother. It should remind us, too, that Jesus has made childhood the standard of value in human life, and has declared that except we are converted, and become as a little child, we can not enter the kingdom of heaven. This child-life about us should cause us to long again for the trust and reverence and hope of our own childhood, and bring us back in the childlike spirit to communion with the Heavenly Father. And association with the aged should remind us of the transitory character of all things earthly, and that it is only the unseen and spiritual virtues which hold their value forever.

Freedom is an angel of summer-time. The harsher seasons have many prison walls that shut us in from perfect liberty of movement. The summer is the free season of the year; we come and go with more ease, with less precaution as to health, and have a better opportunity to follow out the free bent of our desires. That should be an angel to us. God sets us free to do as we will, and it is a type of that perfect freedom of the soul which Christ gives to those who are free from every wicked habit, and who serve God with ready minds and joyous hearts.

XVII.

THE DEVILS PECULIAR TO SUMMER-TIME.

Amos viii. 1.

But summer-time has its devils, also, against which we must be on our guard. One of these is laziness. A cold day makes your step quick. In winter a man must work or starve; he must move lively or freeze. There is a great stimulant in that kind of an atmosphere. The greatest successes of human life have been achieved under the spur of a harsh climate. While the luxury and ease and beauty of summer-time, if we live worthy of them, will all be angels to us, they have also a tendency to make us lazy and sluggish. This is likely to show itself in the lack of church attendance and in neglect of Bible reading, and failure to do earnest Christian work for the help of others. That is one of the devils of summer-time that needs to be watched for. Give way to it, and the summer will impoverish your soul spiritually. You will come to the autumn with less power than you had when the summer opened. Instead of growing you will have become shrunken and shriveled. Take care against the devil of laziness.

Another devil peculiarly alert in the summer is an irritable temper. Some people who are fairly good-humored in winter-time are peppery as a hedgehog when the heat pricks them. There are some business men whose employees go to work with fear and trembling on a hot morning. When the sweat starts, their composure and forbearance seem to melt with it. I suppose one can hardly imagine what added sorrow in the aggregate is piled upon suffering humanity on a hot day through the burden of an irritable temper. A traveler tells how he saw a significant sign painted conspicuously beside the track on an Eastern railroad. It read: "Shut your ashpan." He asked a friend in the car what the meaning of it was. He replied: "That is for the engineer. We are coming to a long wooden bridge, and the company does not want any hot coals from the locomotive dropped on it. They might very easily set the bridge on fire." How many calamities the world would be spared if there were no hot, angry, provoking words dropped about. Who of us has not seen a whole family, or a whole shopful, set by the ears by a few hot, combustible words dropped smoking from angry lips? We ought to remember that we are living among people like ourselves, whom it is very easy to set on fire with angry passions. It would be well if every one of us would heed the warning, "Shut your ashpan."

There is another devil, a good deal like the one last mentioned, which needs to be specially guarded against in summer, and that is the devil of gossip and evil-speaking about one's neighbors. In summer-time, when people congregate together a good deal at picnics, and summer hotels, and in traveling, there is a sort of laxity in regard to a feeling of responsibility which seems to favor the gossiping devil. I was reading recently about tigers, and was interested to note that a man-eating tiger is usually an old beast which has got past the time for catching game, and so seeks an easier game in human beings. But tigers born of a man-eating tigress are always man-eaters, for they get their first lessons in hunting from their mother. A tigress teaches her whelps to hunt as a cat does her kittens, by bringing them live prey to practise upon. An English hunter tells the story of a tigress that was known all over India as the man-eater, who once had given her whelps a live man to play with. She carried off the man from an open hut in the forest where some wood-cutters were sleeping. His companions took refuge in trees, and from their place of safety saw her take the man alive to where the whelps were waiting close by, and lay him down before them. As the man attempted to crawl away the whelps would cling to his legs with teeth and claws, the tigress looking on and purring with pleasure. That is not an exaggerated illustration of the devilish spirit that claws and gnaws at the character of men and women in malicious personal gossip. Beware of that devil.

Irreverence is another demon belonging peculiarly to summer-time and the vacation season. Especially if one is away from home and among strangers, surrounded with new and strange conditions, is there a temptation to throw off the safe, regular habits of church attendance and worship which hold one to a devout life. Unless you resist this devil the summer is likely to bring you a great deal more harm than it does good. Strong natures show themselves as much by remaining faithful to God in unusual situations as anywhere else. The newspaper correspondents and members of Gen. Joseph Wheeler's staff say that during the Santiago campaign the brave old cavalry officer who came out of the war with so much glory never lay down to sleep at night without kneeling beside his cot in prayer, and that the first thing he did when he arose in the morning was reverently to kneel. and thank God for his protection and preservation. If General Wheeler could do that through a trying campaign, with all the excuses for negligence that could be made for his peculiar circumstances, then surely there will be no time during the summer when, on the cars, or on ship board, or in strange cities, or in the forest camping out, it will be necessary for us to yield to the tempter that would lead us to forget God and our daily worship.

We can not afford to forget that our summertime, as well as the more serious seasons of our lives, makes its permanent contribution to the development of character. There was once a rich landlord who cruelly oppressed a poor widow. Her son, then a little boy of eight years, witnessed it. He became a great painter, and painted a likeness of the dark scene. Years afterward he placed it where the cruel man saw it. He recognized himself in the shameful picture, turned pale, trembled in every joint, and offered a large sum to purchase it that he might put it out of sight. And so we may be sure that there is an invisible painter drawing on the canvas of our souls a likeness reflecting all the passions and deeds of our spiritual history on earth. We shall meet our summer-time again, painted in our life picture. God grant that we may so live it with earnest, faithful hearts, with reverence toward God and love toward our fellow man, that when we meet it we shall not be put to confusion!

XVIII.
DISAGREEABLE CHRISTIANS.

Romans xiv. 7-19.

THE Christian life is an ideal life. It is the kind of a life which you can not fulfil by a cold obedience to forms and ceremonies and laws, however strict. One may keep all the law in obedience to the formalities of the letter, and yet, lacking the spirit of Christ, the effect of the life may be thoroughly false. Christianity has the extra of the spirit superimposed upon obedience to the requirements of the law. It is not enough for the Christian to be honest and truthful and pure in his conduct; he must be all these in a gracious spirit fragrant from fellowship with Jesus Christ.

Now there are some particular forms of temptation which the enemy, in order to destroy our influence as Christians, presents to our souls so frequently that it is well worth our while to recall them a moment. One form is that of so-called independence. Some people get a superficial reputation for honesty and genuineness through the brutal way in which they are accustomed to blurt out uncomfortable truths. Such a man is likely to say, "I call things by their right names. There isn't any hypocrisy about me. If I don't like a person I let him know it," and other remarks of that sort. Now such a man is likely to do an enormous amount of harm. He has forgotten that the exhortation to "speak the truth in love" is just as certainly of divine origin as is the requirement to speak the truth at all. And the truth often ceases to be the truth when the love is taken out, and has all the effect of a falsehood.

Another thing must be borne in mind—that we are not always on the witness-stand sworn to tell "the whole truth," and that the Christian spirit will often require us to keep our lips silent and not to speak at all when by speaking we would only put thorns in some one's pillow and do no possible good to any one. To go about advertising every uncomfortable fact, or supposed fact, that we come into possession of is to make ourselves very disagreeable in the community and to make the very name Christian as represented by us a thing to shudder at.

The devil sometimes comes in the garb of purity, and, with the sweet name of holiness on his lips, persuades people that they are holier than anybody else in the church or community, and that other people who do not see things just as they do, and are not able to relate the same sort of experience they can tell about, are not Christians at all, and are in danger of destruction. I remember once in a Western town an old backslider who was so mean and wicked that he had not been inside of a church building for years. I set myself to win that old man back to the Lord, and I visited him, and prayed with him and for him, until, after months of effort, he came back to the church and into joy again as a Christian. But some of these disagreeable saints got hold of him, and led him off on their tack, and it was not six weeks before the old man prayed for me by name in the public service, that I might be saved from the error of my ways and come to pronounce his shibboleth, lest I be damned. A man ought always to be scared about himself when he gets settled in the conviction that he is by far the holiest man in the church. A good Scripture passage for him is that one in the Proverbs, "Seest thou a man wise in his own conceit? there is more hope of a fool than of him." If God has given you a rich experience so that your life is clean and pure, then thrust it out in service and he will honor it. It is not for you to make yourself shine. Go to work, and the Lord will see to it that you shine unto his glory. Humility, not censorious self-assertion, will make your

Christianity agreeable and attractive to people.

Another tack which the devil takes with us is to cause us to look on the black side of the outlook for the church, and on the seamy side of the lives of other Christians. If you meet such a man and congratulate him on the good congregations attending the church services, or on the number who are being converted and the evident growth of spirituality among the people, he will draw down his face as tho he had some inward pain, and remark in a most lugubrious voice and with a hopeless air, "Oh, yes, but the pastor ought to visit the people more than he does; things will all go to pieces unless there is more pastoral work done." And so he goes along, spreading only gloom, and throwing whatever influence he may have on the side of the disagreeable and uncomfortable. If a good deed is done by any one, and the person receives praise in his presence, he always turns the fair robe of life over and shows you the seamy side. Now the Christian way is to see the good that is in people and try to bring that into power and control.

The great cure for each of these disagreeable characteristics is to throw ourselves unreservedly into fellowship with Jesus Christ in helpful service of the Lord. I have always noticed that the man who works the hardest frets the least. The man who works until the perspiration comes out from every pore is the one who has the least to say about the heat. As we put our religious principles and belief and emotions into loving service for our fellow men, we not only please God, but we make our religion attractive and draw attention to Jesus Christ.

XIX.
THE SOURCE OF OUR LOVE FOR CHRIST.

1 John iv. Matthew xxvii. 11-54.

JOHN was an expert on the subject of love, and he says, giving it as his final opinion, that the supreme source of our love for Christ is in our knowledge of the fact that Christ first loved us. To keep ourselves refreshed with this consciousness of Christ's love, I think it is very desirable that we should carefully read, much oftener perhaps than most of us do, the details of the loving sacrifice which Jesus Christ made for us. You tell me that Christ died for me, but that bald statement means very little compared to its meaning when in my imagination I go and kneel beside him in the Garden of Gethsemane, and see the anguish on his face, and watch the bloody sweat-drops swell and fall from his forehead, and hear him as he says, "Not my will, but thine, be done," and know that it is for me that he is willing to suffer so; or when I go with him through the darkness, illuminated only with the torches of the cruel mob of officers that have arrested him, and on to Pilate's judgment hall, and follow him as the crown of thorns is pressed down upon his sensitive brow until the blood starts, and watch them bare his shoulders for the scourging, and see the heavy lash as it falls on his bare back until every time it strikes it seems as tho it were cutting my own quivering flesh, and yet as I look through my tears and see the patience and love in his face I say to myself, "He is bearing it all for me." And then I go with him as they put the heavy cross on his shoulders, and he carries it out and on the road until he sinks under it, not because he is unwilling to carry it to the end, but because the poor, wounded, tired out body has not strength enough in it for the cruel load. And Simon the Cyrenian comes up and is pressed into service, and the Christ follows on until we come to the place of crucifixion. I hide my head, because I can not bear the sight, while the nails are driven through those gentle hands that had quieted the fever in many a burning brow, and while the nails are driven through the feet that had been wet with the grateful tears of the woman who had been ransomed and redeemed by his loving sympathy. But there is suddenly a great shout, and my interest gets the better of my horror, and I lift my eyes to see that the cross with its precious sacrifice has been lifted into its place, and that about the base of it surges a wild and hooting mob. They are abusing him; they are insulting him with harsh and taunting words. They hate him simply because he is good. And then his lips move. The mob is silenced by its curiosity to hear what he will say. They think he will fling back some taunt into their faces. This is the taunt they hear, not addressed to them, but with infinite love in look and divine reverence in expression the gentle, pleading words fall on the ears of the hushed mob, and beyond it to me, "Father, forgive them, for they know not what they do!" How my heart goes out to him as I feel that his suffering, and his prayer, and all the tender self-giving is for me. John knew what he was talking about when he said, "We love him because he first loved us."

I repeat it, we ought to read these incidents of the sacrifice of Jesus Christ more frequently and more thoughtfully than we do. It is not in man to let his imagination run out upon these incidents of the giving of the life of Jesus Christ for us without our own love being aroused in return. And this is all perfectly natural. Love must have incident and detail to hold on to. Love is fed and nourished by kind looks, by tender words, by caresses, by deeds of self-denial, by unusual efforts to please. If you look back over your own friendships you will see that love does not spring up, ready made, at somebody uttering the simple statement, "I love you." There must be a background for love. The eye, the ear, the hand, the lips, and all the windows of the soul must have some evidence of their own, must have some incidents of love for the imagination to dwell upon, for the soul to paint into its inner pictures, which it may study and muse about, while love grows and finally fills the heart with rapture. Now all this must be a type only of what love is between our souls and Christ. Do not for a moment make the great blunder of supposing that your Christian experience is something so entirely different from the rest of your life that it is in any way unnatural to it; it is not. If you love your friend because day after day there have been coming the little happy signals of love that have shown themselves in look and tone and touch and word upon which the mind and heart have seized, then you may be sure that your love for Christ may be refreshed and nourished in the same way. Dwell often upon the details of his loving sacrifice in your behalf and your love will bud and blossom in return.

But if we open our hearts to him in daily prayer and meditation, there will be new expressions of love coming from him to us that will warm our hearts into ever deeper enthusiasm and more precious rapture. He has promised that if we invite him he will come into our hearts, and sit at the daily feast, and we shall sup with him and he will sup with us. In such a heart there goes on a love life between the soul and Jesus Christ that becomes more sweet and beautiful as the years advance, and which can only find complete fruition in heaven.

XX.

HOW TO KEEP CHEERFUL.

Romans xiv. xv. 1-13.

IN the very nature of things an intelligent, genuine Christian must be the happiest person in the world. Discouragement to a Christian must always mean a falling away of faith in some way, for if we really believe that this is God's world and that all things work together for good to them that love him, and we are sure we love him, then we must carry around with us happy faces and hopeful hearts. We have given here by Paul, who was a great expert in hopefulness and happiness, three characteristics of a Christian—righteousness, peace and joy. Two out of three of them indicate cheerfulness. Peace is the bosom of the ocean, and joy the whitecaps which the breezes of life sweeping over the sea awake.

Above everybody else the Christian has a right to look on the bright side of things. The world should not only look beautiful to us because it is beautiful, but because it is an indication of the kindness and love of our Father. It is a failure of faith and a certain indication of practical infidelity when we give way to some temporary defeat and say with gloomy faces that there is no use trying, as everything is against us.

On a very slippery day last winter a young negro was making his way home with a large market basket on his arm, full to the brim with all those hard and ball-like vegetables peculiar to winter. Treading unwaringly on a bit of glare ice he came down suddenly, with a crash that emptied his basket out into the street. Surrounded by garden products, he lay at full length, his head supported on his hand, looking calmly about him. Seeing him still prostrate, a gentleman hurried to him anxiously. "Are you hurt?" "No." "Then why don't you get up?" "'Tain't worth while." A good many of us, having spilled out our little basket of plans and purposes in the street, are as absurd as was that colored man when we say that it is not worth while to continue the struggle because we have caught a fall and find ourselves momentarily confused. After all, this suggests one of the chief methods of keeping cheerful, and that is not to magnify trifling difficulties. It is a sure way to be always filled with misery to exaggerate in the lens of our own imagination, or in our conversation, the difficulties which we all have to meet, and the troubles and sorrows with which we have to contend. Let trifles take their place as trifles and we shall often find that we have nothing but trifles in the way, and that compared to the mammoth mercies of God they are as nothing.

Another way to increase our cheerfulness is to keep the disagreeable things which seem to be our particular cross as much as possible to ourselves. It is not considered in good taste to take one's medicine in public. Why should we take our providential medicine that way? Dr. Scudder well says that there is no greater mistake, so far as the happiness of the world is concerned, than that which is made by those people who go about with their bitter cups and want everybody they meet to take a sip. Some people seem to take a morbid delight in making themselves and other people miserable. If they have no real troubles to worry about they manufacture artificial ones, and their mills never shut down. They grind out just about so much misery whether the market is brisk or dull. They are like old rusty pianos that have not been tuned for years. They are so full of discordant elements that no harmony can be evoked from them. Play on any key and there sounds nothing but a jangle. They whine and sigh, but they never sing. And yet a Christian above all others should be forever singing at the heart.

A sure recipe for cheerfulness is to be always on the alert for some pleasant thing that may happen to us. A washerwoman in a miserable tenement-house was asked how she kept singing in her disheartening surroundings. "Oh, because there is always a breeze in the alley." She might have said it was because she had a singing heart within her. To every such soul God giveth songs in the night.

Kate Sanborn tells of an old lady of her acquaintance, eighty-three years of age, who is famous among all who know her for her happy cheerfulness. One day when she was choked by a bread crumb at the table, she said to the frightened waiter as soon as she could regain her breath: "Never mind if that did go down the wrong way. A great many good things have gone down the right way this winter."

This dear old saint is always seeking to keep others from being unhappy, and when she was parting with her son for the winter, she said: "Well, John, I want to know before you go just what you have left me in your will." This little joke turned a tear into a smile.

One day when quite ill, she was still so bright and hopeful that a friend exclaimed: "Grandma, I do believe you would laugh if you were dying!"

"Well," she said, "so many folks go to the Lord

with a long face, I guess he will be glad to see me come to him smiling!"

Having a consciousness of God's presence and of his kindness to us, and consideration for the condition of others, so that our lives run out in fellowship, sunning ourselves in the joy and love not only of the Lord but of our friends, I am sure we shall find abundant sources of cheerfulness.

A namesake of mine, Mr. J. Linnæus Banks, has written a little poem entitled "What I Live For." If we could enter into the spirit of his verse I am sure it would help us all into the way of cheerfulness.

"I live for those who love me,
　Whose hearts are kind and true;
For the heaven that smiles above me,
　And awaits my spirit, too;
For all human ties that bind me,
For the task by God assigned me,
For the bright hopes yet to find me,
　And the good that I can do.

"I live to learn their story
　Who suffered for my sake;
To emulate their glory,
　And follow in their wake;
Bards, patriots, martyrs, sages,
The heroes of all ages,
Whose deeds crowd history's pages,
　And Time's great volume make.

"I live to hold communion,
  With all that is divine,
To feel there is a union
  'Twixt nature's heart and mine;
To profit by affliction,
Reap truth from fields of fiction,
Grow wiser from conviction,
  Fulfil God's grand design.

"I live to hail that season
  By gifted ones foretold,
When men shall live by reason,
  And not alone by gold;
When man to man united,
And every wrong thing righted,
The whole world shall be lighted,
  As Eden was of old.

"I live for those who love me,
  For those who know me true,
For the heaven that smiles above me,
  And awaits my coming, too;
For the cause that lacks assistance,
For the wrong that needs resistance,
For the future in the distance,
  And the good that I can do."

XXI.
THE IMPERISHABLE MAN WITHIN.

1 Corinthians iv.

THAT the outward man is temporary, perishable, and uncertain, we have abundant evidence. Most of us are already taking medicine to patch up the holes in this temporary house in which we live. In spite of all the patching we can do, it will steadily grow old and become more and more uncomfortable. The troublesome thing about the outward man is that he will not perish peaceably. He is a great grumbler. Through toothache and earache and rheumatism and dyspepsia he is perpetually making us know that he is badly off and will not last a great while. It is wise to take just as good care of him as we can, so that he shall not interfere with the work and happiness of the imperishable inward man who is in for the long race of eternity.

Some people make the fatal mistake of putting all their attention on this outward man, planning and working day and night to lay up treasures to clothe and feed and coddle him, while the infinitely more splendid and noble man within is left to starve. Dr. Aitkin, the English evangelist, says that a very rich man was once showing him through his house, and, after scaling a high tower, pointed in a northerly direction, and said: "As far as your eye can reach that is all mine."

"Is that so?" said his friend.

"Yes. Now turn this way; that is also mine."

"Indeed!" said the minister.

"Now look southerly—that is all mine; and westerly—that is mine also. In fact, on all four points of the compass, as far as the eye can reach, it is all mine."

Dr. Aitkin, looking at him, paused and said: "Yes; I see you have land on all four quarters; but"—pointing his finger upward—"what have you in that direction?"

The man who was rich in goods for the outer man, but who was a spiritual bankrupt, blushed and stammered, and had no answer.

The best thing about the imperishable inward man is that all his strength and beauty may be renewed day by day. Love and hope and faith, the great abiding factors in this world, are capable of constant renewal. Their great source is in God, who is love, and who keepeth faith forever, and who is able to inspire hope in us under all circumstances. He who sent his angel to watch over Elijah under the juniper-tree in the desert, when he was worn out and discouraged, feeding him and comforting him as a mother does a fretful child, until his glorious strength came back again, has just as tender care and sympathy for us.

It is well to notice that to keep this inward man strong he must have daily feeding. He must have his meals regularly. Paul says the spiritual life should be renewed "day by day." There is the serious mistake which many people make. Some people go on religious sprees, as it were. They have spells when they go to church a great deal, hear many sermons and give themselves up much to absorbing religious teaching; and then they drop away from it and have long seasons of seeming indifference. It is impossible that such a person should be a healthy Christian. You might as well expect a man to have a healthy body who gorged himself for a week with rich food, and then fasted for a month. I remember in my boyhood a man who was a great singer, and when he would get with religious people and get to singing the old hymns he would become very happy, and for a time seem to enjoy himself religiously very much. He used to have a season of this sort at camp-meeting time. Any one seeing him then would have believed him to be the most devotedly pious man in the community. But between times, in his business life, he seemed to forget his religion. An irreverent neighbor used to say that the only way to ever get him to heaven would be to take him to a camp-meeting and let him sing himself happy, and then kill him. Alas! that there are so many whose religious history is of such erratic and irregular sort that it is of no beauty or power as a religious force in the community. But we need not live such lives as that. We may renew our spiritual life day by day so that the spiritual graces will be ever beautiful and abundant in our living, and their influence will be gracious and helpful to our fellow men.

The passing of the years has no power to make feeble or decrepit the imperishable man within. Dr. Henry M. Field, the editor of *The Evangelist*, who is over eighty years young, recently said to the Christian Endeavorers of the country: "I have been young and now am old. I have had experience of life at every stage, from youth to the noontide of manhood, till now I am getting into the twilight of age. Perhaps you would like to ask how it seems to be growing old. Is there not a slow decay, in which body and mind grow weaker and life grows poorer? I know not how it is with others, but for myself life grows richer every day as I get into the higher altitudes. It is as when I was on the Alps or the Himalayas, from which I looked down into the valleys of Switzerland or far away to the plains of India. You who are just entering upon life inhale the dewy freshness of the morning, and feel an exhilaration as you start in the race. But the sweetest hour in the day is that of sunset. And much as you may love life, there is nothing in it quite equal to the holy calm of the tired pilgrim when at last he comes into the Land of Beulah, and is in full view of the Delectable Mountains."

What a glorious thing it is to grow old like that! Yet such an old age is possible for every one of us who shall remain to so great an age. But to be happy and strong and splendid in old age we must begin in youth to refresh and renew the imperishable man within who alone can glorify the later years of life.

XXII.

THE ART OF RECEIVING GOOD ADVICE.

1 Samuel xxv. 26-33.

DAVID had been insulted by a man named Nabal, and in his anger had determined to take vengeance into his own hands. As he was marching to punish the churlish old rancher he met Abigail, the wife of Nabal, who came to meet him on the way and reason with him in regard to his proposed vengeance. She urges upon him that, while his anger at Nabal is certainly justifiable, it is unworthy of a man whom God has ordained to so great a career as that promised to David to stain his hands with blood in a quarrel with so insignificant and mean a man as Nabal. And she draws a picture of the days that are to come when all the enemies that stand against David shall be overthrown, and he shall have come into his kingdom. Then says this wise woman, in substance: "When you have come into your own, and reign in undisputed sway over the land, how much happier you will be to remember that in these trying years of adversity you were kind and forbearing, and refused to wreak vengeance by your own hand."

One of the greatest characteristics of David and one of the greatest reasons of his prosperity in life was that he was a man who could be advised. He was impulsive, and sometimes overcome by temptation, but he was never mulish or stubborn in a bad path. So, instead of gritting his teeth like a fool and going on to his folly whether or no, David listened to what she had to say, and being convinced that the course marked out by her was the wiser, he frankly admitted it, and said: "Blessed be the Lord God of Israel, which sent thee this day to meet me: and blessed be thy advice, and blessed be thou, which has kept me this day from coming to shed blood, and from avenging myself with mine own hand."

It is a characteristic of great souls that they are easily advised. The greater the man, the greater his willingness to learn: the greater his desire to know all the facts in the case and to come to a wise conclusion concerning them. Whenever you see a man who thinks he knows it all, and is too wise to learn from any one unless it is some one in a higher position than himself, you may be sure that however great he may be in some ways, you have in that self-sufficient wisdom an indication of narrowness. We should always be ready and quick to learn from any source.

It is, however, very important to choose carefully our advisers; no one in this world is wise enough to go alone without advice. Solomon was the wisest man that ever lived, and yet he says, "With the well advised is wisdom." Often when a man is running for a great office, people take into account who his advisers will be if he comes into the position. His conduct, it is understood, will largely depend upon his advisers. The greatest interest is always taken in the choosing of a cabinet by a king or a president, for upon the advice of these counselors the conduct of the ruler of the nation will largely depend. Our individual lives are much like that. Every one of us has a cabinet of advisers, tho we may be all unconscious of it.

Now the Christian idea of living is that Jesus Christ should be the Prime Minister, the Chief Counselor, in every Christian life. One of the names given to Christ in prophecy was that of Counselor, and we should take him as the counselor and adviser supreme in our daily lives.

How simple and straightforward was the advice which Jesus gave to some of the people who talked with him when he lived in human form here on the earth! Take his advice about greed and anxiety to lay hold upon everything within reach, and to worry about it when riches did not come rapidly. How he pointed his friends to the growing lilies, with their beauty and their perfume; to the birds gathering their food with each morning's bounty. And he said to them, God takes care of these, and certainly they are not his creatures more than you are. God is more interested in you, his children, than he is in birds and flowers; go on, then, about your work, seek first to be good and do your duty, and God will take care of these incidental things.

No one has ever given such good advice in regard to the great fact that possession is not necessary in order to get happiness out of the good things of life. Hear Jesus giving advice one day: "A man's life consisteth not in the abundance of the things which he possesseth." We are always being tempted to think we can never be happy unless we can get into our possession whatever charms or attracts us; but Christ taught that joy and blessing from God's good gifts come to the heart that is right and true, and the soul that is open to receive, often without possession. You do not need to pluck every flower you see and put it in a vase in order to enjoy it. You ought to be thankful that other people take care of the grounds where some of the trees spread their shade and some of the flowers bloom whose beauty and fragrance refresh your soul day by day. If we can not possess the things that are beautiful and attractive to us, let us thank God that we are able to appreciate them, and rejoice in the beauty that gives us gladness. There are people who spoil all the joys of friendship through jealousy about their friends. How much wiser to revel in the sweet gift of God in our friend, and rejoice that our friend is great enough to give helpfulness and blessings to other souls as well as to us. Indeed, Christ's great advice about life is that character and not conditions make or unmake our happiness. It is a great lesson, and we need Jesus to walk with us day by day, and impress his divine advice upon our hearts.

If we will accept his counsel, Christ will lead us, and inspire and comfort us to the end. David said to God, "Thou shalt guide me with thy counsel, and afterward receive me to glory." So if we open our hearts to Christ in friendship, and are sensitive to listen to his advice, he will guide us safely through life's toil and struggle, through dark days and bright days, to old age and beyond it to the heaven that is to be. The secret of immortal youth is to live in this counsel and fellowship with Christ who came that we might have life, and have it more abundantly. Whittier, the Christ-loving Quaker poet, when close to the end, in those days when he was burning "driftwood," but found the fire warm enough to keep his heart young, wrote his last poem to Oliver Wendell Holmes, in which he said:

> "Far off and faint as the echoes of a dream
> The songs of boyhood seem.
> Yet on our autumn boughs, unflown with spring,
> The evening thrushes sing.
>
> "The hour draws near, howe'er delayed and late,
> When at the eternal gate
> We leave the words and works we call our own,
> And lift void hands alone
>
> "For love to fill. Our nakedness of soul
> Brings to that gate no toll:
> Giftless, we come to him who all things gives,
> And live because he lives."

XXIII.
THE BLESSINGS OF HOPE.

Romans viii. 13–39.

PAUL in this chapter says some splendid things about hope. So great is his estimate of it that he declares it to be the essential link in the chain of salvation. It is hope that inspires the heart to trust Christ and follow him through evil as well as good report.

A mechanical engineer of Lemberg, Austria, has discovered a strange and very subtle matter which he has called "electroid," because of its affinity with electricity. Electroid, produced by a special apparatus built by the inventor, is obtained by the dissolution of certain matters under the influence of the electric current. It makes a noise, and at the same time a refreshing scent and cool breeze are experienced. This discovery induced Mr. Rychnowski, the inventor, to make a machine capable of refreshing the air to such a degree that those present during the experiment had the feeling that the window was open, altho this was not the case. The commission appointed by the Austrian government to investigate this discovery reported that, under the influence of electroid, plants grow rapidly, and the buds of flowers unclose while one is looking at them. Electroid annihilates microbes, and thus preserves organic matter.

Hope is a divine electroid; it is an atmosphere in which the noblest buds of human life open in blossom. It inspires men with new courage, and preserves the health and strength of the soul. No man is ever defeated while hope remains.

Another great thing which Paul says about hope is when he gives it as the foundation of patience. He says, "If we hope for that we see not, then do we with patience wait for it." Hope is the mother of patience. And patience, tho often held to be a humble sort of virtue, has a vast amount to do with the beauty and happiness of life. Hope inspires us with two kinds of patience. One kind is that which enables us to keep a level head and a sweet temper under trying circumstances. If you take away from a man all hope that things can ever be better, and then put him into the midst of some hornets' nest of personal annoyance, you will make a madman of him; but if you inspire a man's heart with hope that the present annoyance is temporary, and is a very insignificant thing when compared with the great victories of life which are yet to come, his hope makes him patient, and gives him power to control his temper and refrain from petulance, or anger, or despair. It was a patience born of that sort of hope that enabled Paul to say in the midst of the great trials that beset him: "Our light affliction, which is but for a moment, worketh for us a far more exceeding and eternal weight of glory; while we look not at the things which are seen, but at the things which are not seen: for the things which are seen are temporal; but the things which are not seen are eternal. For we know that if our earthly house of this tabernacle were dissolved, we have a building of God, an house not made with hands, eternal in the heavens." If a man has only one house, and the roof is beginning to leak, and he has no hope of patching it up, you can understand the annoyance and the terror that will come to him. But if hope present to his view another house, grander and more splendid and more comfortable than anything he has yet known, he can endure the leaky roof for a few days with patience.

Hope is the mother of still another sort of patience, which makes us brave to endure hardship and struggle not only because they will soon pass away, but because in them we have the opportunity to do good and to come into fellowship with Jesus Christ our Savior.

One of the greatest elements of Christianity is its hopefulness. Sin is the mother of despair; it robs the soul of hope. It is easy to win a man to Christ when you have plucked his feet out of the "slough of despond" into which sin has led him and in which he flounders. Get the heart inflated and inspired with the great hope of forgiveness of sin and purity of life through Jesus Christ, and salvation comes easily after that. There is another passage which says that the man who gets such a hope in his soul "purifieth himself." The old rags of sin and evil appetite and wicked habits are thrown away when the new robe of righteousness is made possible to us through hope in Christ.

Let us give hope full play in our lives. It will cleanse us, it will inspire us, and finally it will be an anchor to the soul that will hold steadfast in the harbor to which we shall come in safety and peace at last.

XXIV.
WALKING WITH GOD.

Genesis v. 24.   Jude 14.   Hebrews ix. 5.

HE is a great artist who can sketch a human portrait and condense the prophecy of a lifetime of public effort into sixty-four words, and yet make the picture so clear and unique that it stands out, in a great portrait-gallery like the Bible, full of abiding interest and comfort to generation after generation. Still more marvelous is it when three artists have each a single stroke at the picture. Only sixty-four words, and yet what a strong, noble figure they cause to stand before the mind and heart! I would rather have those sixty-four words as my biography and as my monument than all the volumes that have been written about Cæsar, Alexander, and Napoleon combined.

The great characteristic of Enoch's life was that he "walked with God." What a comforting picture of the tenderness and sympathy of divine fellowship is proffered to us in the Bible!—and we are assured that it is within the reach of every child of

God. We do not go walking with every chance stranger whom we meet, but usually with those of our more intimate acquaintances and choice friends. The figure used indicates a relation at once confidential and sympathetic. And that is the relation we ought to hold to our heavenly Father. We often cheat our souls of one of the sweetest comforts of life by thinking of God as seated high above us, upon a great white throne—white like snow, indicating coldness and dignity. Thus while we admire him, and are grateful for his mercy and goodness, and have a deep desire to please him, we miss the thought of tender fellowship which is illustrated to us in the Word of God in many charming and beautiful pictures. God is represented as walking in the garden in the cool of the day and holding conversation with Adam and Eve even after their sin. When Abraham dwelt at Mamre in the desert, God came to him in the guise of a weary traveler, and received food and water from the hand of his servant. And Jesus Christ gives us a most comforting view of our relation to God by declaring that we may enter into a yoke-fellowship, walking side by side, pulling the same load, and sharing both the food and burden of the divine life.

A distinguished minister was entertained at the house of a very prominent man, who was known far and wide not only for his great learning, but for his deep and sincere religious experience. The visitor was very curious to learn as much as possible of the inner life of this man whose spiritual force made so profound an impression on all who came in contact with him. One evening, after he had bidden his host good-night, he left the door of his room ajar that he might hear, if possible, the evening devotions of the good man in the room adjoining. He was successful. After a little time the saint put aside his books and the work he had in hand; then after reading his Bible he knelt and offered this simple prayer, "Lord Jesus, things are still just the same between us," and retired for the night. What a sweet and intimate fellowship with God is suggested by that brief prayer! There is no need of many words of intercession or entreaty or explanation when one walks day by day in such simple and unbroken harmony with God.

Enoch, like all men who walk with God, found constant and abiding joy in spiritual things. Those things which are pleasing to God are the natural surroundings, the native atmosphere, of such a soul. Paul says that the carnal mind is enmity against God, and can not if it would please him. People who are not Christians often wonder how Christian people can find happiness and joy in reading the Bible, in prayer, and in spiritual conversation—things which to them seem dull and uninteresting. But to the man or woman who has been born into the kingdom of Christ, prayer, praise, and Christian fellowship form the joyous atmosphere of the daily life. The soul breathes in such an atmosphere the very breath of heaven.

Throughout my boyhood and young manhood, over in the Northwestern mountains, in many a mountain climb and fishing excursion I have watched with most friendly interest a little bird which I think is not known in the East, called the water-ouzel. Many times in the deep, dark cañons one's only companion is this little ouzel, that always lives about waterfalls and cataracts. He spends all his life in an atmosphere of flashing spray and the noisy turmoil of falling water. John Muir, the California mountaineer and naturalist, says of him: " He is the mountain-stream's own darling, the humming-bird of blooming waters, loving rocky ripple-slopes and sheets of foam as a bee loves flowers, as a lark loves sunshine." The mother ouzel always makes her nest on some rocky ledge, where it is constantly receiving the gentle spray from some waterfall, so that the moss out of which the nest is made is ever kept fresh and green. Indeed, I have seen the nest built back of the fall itself, where it seemed impossible that eggs could hatch out because of the constant dampness. The little ouzel pecking his way to life in that moss nest is rarely, if ever, in the course of his whole career, beyond the reach of the music of running and falling water. The songs that he sings—and he sings them very sweetly all the year round, winter as well as summer—are all songs of the water, taught him by the cataracts. This little bird fairly lives in the water. He not only nests near it, but he gets all his food from it, for he can not only dive in the water like a duck, but he is able to walk on the bottom of the stream, and can even fly under the rapid running water of a mountain torrent. A naturalist relates a beautiful story of this interesting little bird. On one occasion he was camping out beside a slender stream up in the Rocky Mountains. After drinking, he threw the water out of his cup into the stream, when instantly an ouzel flew up as if to catch the drops. Curious to see if that were really his object, he threw more water, and was delighted to see that every time he did so the bird flew up into the falling shower, evidently enjoying the sprinkle on its plumage.

It seems to me that this little mountain-bird is a beautiful illustration of the way the Christian who in humility and faith walks with God comes to find the very atmosphere he loves to breathe in doing those things that please God. The man whose heart and affections are set upon the world, and who breathes an atmosphere of selfishness and sensuality, can not understand how this can be, any more than a mocking bluejay can understand the water-ouzel's fondness for the roar of the waterfall or a plunge in its white spray. And, thank God, as the little ouzel is able to sing its sweet song all the year round—as cheerfully when the blizzards of December chill other birds and send them shivering to some warmer clime, or when the dusty heat of the summer-time parches to silence other throats, as in the most brilliant and blossoming days of spring—so the man who walks in fellowship with God can sing all the year round. He can sing in all seasons and in all weathers. Give him only the assurance of God's presence, and no matter how dark the day or how lowering the threatenings of trouble, his soul will sing its song of confiding trust.

XXV.
SPIRITUAL CULTURE.

Hosea xiv.

THIS is the time of year when culture speaks for itself in the green world of the fields and the gardens. The plowing, the harrowing, the fertilizing, and all the toil of autumn, winter, and spring, all the hours and days of anxious planning, all the intelligence brought to bear by the farmer in the choosing of machinery, the selection of certain seed for certain soil, and the grafting of trees—all this is coming back now in wheat and barley, in peas and potatoes, in apples and pears, and in all the glory of the fragrant blossoms.

But there is another kind of gardening, a higher form of culture, going on all the while in the minds and hearts of every one of us. What kind of culture are we giving to the spiritual possibilities of our souls? That is a question of the very greatest interest. Paul says, "Ye are God's tilled land." If we submit ourselves to him with loving obedience he will superintend the culture of our spiritual life, and will bring forth as a result something far more beautiful and splendid than we had dared hope for. Through the mouth of Hosea the Lord says he will be "as the dew" upon his people. The dew comes in the dry season when the showers are lacking. God does not forget those who trust him in times of drought. His dew will keep the green branches from withering and fainting in the midst of the summer.

It is a characteristic of Christian character that it is a growing, ever-enlarging character. "He shall grow as the lily." The lily grows rapidly and blooms in fragrance; so those who trust God shall have abundant growth.

The Christian is a well-rooted man in his convictions and confidence. "He shall cast forth his roots as Lebanon." Lebanon was the place of the great cedar forest. Those tall, splendid trees had great roots to run deep underground and hold the tree secure in time of storm. The roots serve still another purpose: they run far down below the surface of the soil, and act as pumps to tap the hidden streams of water in "the deep that coucheth beneath," thus giving life to the tree during the long summer-time. So a Christian's roots of faith run down deep into the soil of God's promises; they tap streams of communion with God, of fellowship with Jesus Christ. When all earthly promises fail, the Christian's hope is not destroyed, because of the comfort which is drawn from that hidden confidence in God. When the winds of opposition blow hardest, the soul stands in strong assurance that God is able to keep his children and to bring them off victorious.

The Christian character is most beautiful and fragrant. "His beauty shall be as the olive-tree, and his smell as Lebanon." That is a mingled metaphor. The olive-tree is beautiful in the graceful drooping of its branches and the glossy coloring of its leaves, while the branches of the cedar are famous for their fragrance. There is a picture of us as we ought to be—as we may be. In the heart of God there is cherished an ideal of us that is beautiful and fragrant like that. Oh, that we might realize it! The world needs so much to rest its languid eyes on the beauty of Christian character. It needs so much to be refreshed by the fragrance of unselfish deeds and Christlike conduct.

Such a life is always useful; people that are faint and ready to die, coming under the restful shadow of such a character, revive again. What a blessed thing it is to live in such fellowship with the divine mind that the simplicity of Christ's spirit in us shall cheer the fainting, shall inspire the discouraged, and shall comfort those that mourn!

XXVI.

THE GOOD AND THE BAD WORLDLINESS.

1 John ii. 1-17.

THERE are a number of places in the Bible where the "world" and "worldliness" are spoken of in a spirit of condemnation, and Christians are warned as to being drawn away by them. It is, however, certainly not meant to be taught by these passages that one can not live a holy life while engaged in the ordinary worldly pursuits. The life of Jesus is an abiding proof against this. Every attempt to hide oneself away from the ordinary obligations and duties of the life of the world in order thereby to insure purity has been a failure. Such a life is a starved, dwarfed life. The meaning is, I think, made clear in these words of John, where he explains that the danger of worldliness comes from the pride of life, the lust of the eye, and the love for those things that are constantly perishing. It is not life itself that is condemned, but pride; it is not the beauties which the eye beholds, but lust;

it is not that we are to shut ourselves out of the enjoyment of things that are transient, but that we shall hold them at their relative value, and not set our heart on them to the loss of those things that will last forever. In other words, the worldly man, in this sense which is under condemnation, is one who sets his heart on the binding of the book, and cares nothing at all for the inspiring truths the volume itself may hold. It is cherishing the husk while the ear of corn is thrown away. It is frittering one's life away on things as transient as blossoming poppies while great values are lost.

Mr. Moody tells of a young couple who on commencing to keep house started to keep an account of their family expenses. After a few months the young husband said to his wife: "Darling, I'll spend the evening at home to-night, and we will look over the account together." The young husband found frequent entries like this: "G. K. W., one dollar and a half"; and a little later on, "G. K. W., two dollars"; and after a little, "G. K. W., three dollars." Becoming a little suspicious, he demanded, "Who is this 'G. K. W.' you have spent so much on?" "Oh," said she, "I never could make the accounts come out right, so I lumped all together that wouldn't balance, and called it G. K. W.—Goodness Knows What!"

There seems to be a large number of people who

spend their time and nervous energy on "goodness knows what;" and after it is passed it is like a tale that is told, because there has been no great purpose, no sublime spirit, no real abiding achievement. The present world, with its imperative duties as well as its illusive temptations, is so very near to us and so very insistent, as well as persistent, in its attraction that unless we cultivate our spiritual nature by Bible reading and prayer and meditation on religious things, we shall find ourselves in the condition of that great old Scotch preacher, Dr. Chalmers, when he said: "I am bustled out of my spirituality."

Some of you remember from your childhood the old story of "Sindbad," the sailor of the Indian Ocean, and how the magnetic rock rose above the surface of the placid waters. While hardly being aware of it, Sindbad's vessel was attracted toward it little by little. Silently, one after another, the bolts were drawn out of the ship's side by the imperceptible attraction of the magnetic rock. After a while every bolt and clamp were unloosed. Suddenly, unexpectedly, the whole ship—bulwark, mast, and spars—tumbled into ruin upon the sea. When the sailors awoke it was only to find themselves lost beyond rescue. The dangers from worldly pleasures and worldly ambitions are like the dangers to those sailors in the old story of

"Sindbad." Unless we are watchful, one after another of the bolts which hold our spiritual life compact and solid and secure will be drawn out. Usually the first bolt to go is a stated time of secret prayer; then the daily reading of one or more chapters of the Bible. Perhaps the attendance on prayer-meeting goes next; then it is easy to drop Sunday-school attendance. The religious paper is dropped off from the family reading; a carelessness becomes apparent as to regularity of attendance even on the Sunday services. And all this time the man is not alarmed. He sleeps on until, suddenly, under the spell of some unexpected emergency or unusual temptation, his whole ship of religious faith, which has been gradually weakening all the while, goes to pieces and he finds himself swamped in sin. God forbid that it should ever be so with any of us! But if it is not to be so it must be because we refresh and strengthen our lives daily by communion with God and spiritual fellowship with his people.

As some one has said, religion is not the stop of an organ to be pulled out for Sunday and then pushed in for the rest of the week. It is rather the life and spirit which is to pervade all the music of daily doings. True religion is the spirit of Christ in our hearts. And just as Jesus was as ready with deeds of healing, words of love, and outpouring of prayer to God on one day as another, so we are to show forth our Christianity day by day.

A little girl in Rhode Island expressed a great deal in her evening prayer. After the usual "Now I lay me down to sleep," she continued: "Good-by, God; good-by, Jesus. I'm going to Boston to-morrow." I'm afraid there are many people who, while they would be shocked to put it just that way, yet practically say good-by to their thoughts of God and their obligations to him when they enter upon their daily business, political, or social engagements.

It is the glory of our Christianity that it is neither transient nor temporary, and if we give it the full right of way in our hearts, its upspringing fountain will send forth living streams to refresh and make fertile every field of our human achievement.

XXVII.
THE EVOLUTION OF THE SHIRK.

Ephesians ii.

THE splendid figure with which this chapter closes, which compares the church to a growing temple, and every member of it to a stone which fits into its place and helps to make strong and beautiful the wall of the Lord's house, is full of teaching. To get the real meaning and the full power of the illustration we must think of a building in which every individual stone is alive and full of consciousness of its importance and value in the building, and mastered by an obedient love for the plan of the architect, so that with loving consciousness it seizes hold upon every stone about it to help strengthen the wall of the temple. Or we might conceive of a building in which every stone was a magnet, sending forth invisible but powerful attraction which joins strength with the magnetism in every other stone that touches it, so that by the inherent magnetic quality the stones are held together in harmonious purpose.

Now that was Paul's idea of the building up of the kingdom of God in the earth; and whatever else you may say of Paul, you are compelled to admit that he was a great spiritual architect. The world has never seen his superior as an organizer. He knew how to gather men together and hurl them in united phalanx against the foe. And his idea of the church was that every man should regard himself as a living, vital, essential part of its power, and give himself completely—as completely as a stone does to the wall—to the great purpose in hand.

Now we all know what happens when a stone shirks its duty in the wall of a building. It may mean that the building is only disfigured and marred, or it may mean that it comes tumbling down to the ground. Surely the strength and beauty of the whole depend upon the fidelity, the stability, and the harmony of every part. If this is true of the dead walls of a temple, it is true with far greater emphasis of an architectural creation constructed of sensitive human souls, where the strength depends upon the magnetic sympathy and fellowship and love of the parts one for another, and their devotion and fidelity to the great Architect whose tender wisdom is over all.

We put the emphasis so much on the sins of commission that I think the sin of shirking, which is usually the omitting to do what we ought, is often looked upon as a very light and venial offense. But we certainly have no warrant to so regard it in the teaching of Scripture. Do you remember, in Deborah's great song, of the curse which God put in her mouth for a little town up among the hills— one that simply stayed at home and minded its own business, and did not send its quota of soldiers when the rest went out to war against Sisera? "Curse ye Meroz, said the angel of the Lord, curse ye bitterly the inhabitants thereof; because they came not to the help of the Lord, to the help of the Lord against the mighty." Meroz has disappeared from the map of the world, but it retains an unenviable immortality as the shirker. It stands as a symbol of the shirk through all the centuries. Now there are in every church and in every community people who shirk their part of the work. They talk well, and no doubt have good impulses occasionally; but when it comes to facing the music, and sharing the self-sacrifice, and really going out to battle for the Lord, they stay at home and take good care of their scalps. The church could more than double its power to-morrow if it were not for the shirks. These people always have an excuse when the subscription-paper comes around. The collection somehow is always taken when it is a bad time for them. If it is necessary for somebody to do an unpopular thing for righteousness' sake, there are always lots of good reasons why their names should not be known in it. But if there is any glory gained afterward, they are as ready as this town of Meroz was to take their part of the spoil.

Now I am sure that none of us want to be shirks. And if any of us are shirks, we would like to get out of it and become something stronger and better. But our theme, which we must not forget, is "The Evolution of the Shirk." What causes the shirk? what are the elements that create him? Fear is at the bottom, first of all. The inhabitants of Meroz were a timid lot, and so they stayed at home. And so, many good people really think they are too timid, too bashful, of too retiring a disposition to stand out openly in their place and take the brunt of outspoken friendship for Christ and his cause. If you give way to that fear you will become a shirk.

Another cause is a false humility. People say, I can do so little that I will only be in the way. No doubt the people of Meroz said, "If we could send a thousand men, like some larger towns, they should go, and how proud we would be of them. But we have only twenty-five fighting men at best, and our little hill company would be laughed at." And so they stayed at home. And some of you are making the same blunder. You imagine that if you could do a great deal you would do it for the Lord, while at the same time you are selfishly keeping back from him the little you could do. Let us away with all such false humility as that! Bring what you have to God's altar. He will take it and use it at the right place, and bring victories that you never dreamed of out of it.

Laziness is another prime cause for the creation of the shirk. People like their ease. They selfishly let the duty go undone rather than disturb their quietness and peace. But how unworthy that is of us, when we remember how Jesus our Savior put aside all the glory of heaven and came down to suffer not only hunger and thirst and weariness—that is easy—but insult and abuse and loneliness and heartbreak, that he might comfort and save us. When we are tempted to shirk our duty, let us think of him, and come back again to our strength.

XXVIII.

HOMESICKNESS.

Hebrews xi. 1-16.

THERE is a proverb which says, "Home is where the heart is," and there is probably no proverb more true than that. It takes more than a few thousand bricks, or a few thousand cubic feet of stone, or a pile of lumber thrown into architectural form and beauty, to make a home. Fine carpets, beautifully figured wallpaper, rare pictures, luxurious furniture, tables loaded with appetizing things to eat and drink, libraries full of books, musical instruments—all these may furnish and adorn and help to give comfort to a home, but not all of them together, no matter how lavishly bestowed, can constitute a home in themselves. There is many a mansion so beautiful and splendid that its owners are envied by the people who watch them come and go from such palatial quarters, which, nevertheless, has not about it the first element of a real home.

On the other hand, there is many a log cabin up

in the mountains, many a cottage down in the quiet valley, many a humble little flat in the town, where the furnishings are meager, where the artificial attractions are few, where the food is plain, and where every comfort is at the cost of exacting toil, that is nevertheless a home in the noblest and holiest and sweetest sense of the word. It is the abode of love and peace; it is a place where men and women and children, coming weary from the day's exertions, find in each other's love and fellowship an elixir of life under whose spell body and mind and heart are rested and refreshed, and every morning's sun finds in them new courage for the mission of life.

Such a home has about it a divine attraction, whether rich or humble in its appointments. There is about it a magnetism that draws the thoughts of the heart toward it with longing wherever its happy dwellers may be called upon to wander. It is this longing of the soul for home and for its accustomed fellowship that we call "homesickness." It is the most tender and sacred sickness known to mankind, and is ofttimes most painful, and sometimes fatal even to life itself.

It is this homesickness which makes every young man and young woman coming from the country or the village into a large city a possible prize for the alert and earnest Christian church. Homesickness is such a tender disease that whoever shows sympathy and offers fellowship at such a time is likely to arouse large return in interest in the homesick heart. The haunts of sin know this, and hence there are always hovering about trappers for these devilish places, watching for the young man or the young woman whose heart is sore with absence from home, and aching with loneliness; and many a young person has yielded to the fascinations of sinful temptation at a time like that who would have been impregnable to assault under other circumstances. God help the church to have smiling face and open arms and gracious fellowship for the lonely and the homesick!

Now this homesickness is a type of that higher homesickness, the longing for complete fellowship with Christ. And as one goes on in life there is a deeper longing for a final home in heaven where one may rejoice in the presence of the heavenly Father, and be reunited with the loved ones that have gone before.

The writer of the eleventh chapter of Hebrews, which is called "the roll-call of the heroes of the faith," declares that the early patriarchs, who were seeking while on earth a promised land and yet found themselves "strangers and pilgrims on the earth," were comforted with a glimpse of the better country still, beyond the Jordan of death, where

"God is not ashamed to be called their God," and where "he hath prepared for them a city." It was this that comforted Enoch as he walked with God in those wicked days, and kept his righteousness and his faith in spite of all the sinfulness of the world. It was this that nerved Noah to build his ark, and this that inspired Abraham to go forth with confidence, even tho he did not know where he was going, and made him content to dwell in tents in a strange country. It was the longing of his heart for the heavenly country and the faith that he had that God would bring him to it in peace.

The more we love God, the more faithfully we serve him, the truer we are to his worship, the more hospitality we show toward him and the causes and the people dear to him, the deeper this heavenly longing, and the greater power this magnetism gets on us to draw us onward and upward toward the skies. If, like Abraham, we keep open house for God's angels, we may dwell as he did in the desert places of trial in perfect peace, for we shall know that the desert is not our home, and that these earthly tents are pitched, every night, a day's march nearer to our abiding rest.

"O sweet and blessed country,
The home of God's elect!

Homesickness.

O sweet and blessed country
  That eager hearts expect!
Jesus, in mercy bring us
  To that dear land of rest;
Who art, with God the Father,
  And Spirit, ever blest."

XXIX.

MY GOSPEL.

Romans ii. 1-16.

THE first chapter of Paul's letter to the Romans is one of the darkest pictures of human life where the heart has been given over to sinful lusts that was ever portrayed in human language. After writing that chapter concerning the vile and monstrous condition of heathenism, it is not astonishing that Paul should turn with great relief and thanksgiving to the Gospel of Christ which had been committed to him. He turned to the good news in Christ Jesus which had brought such comfort and blessing into his own life with a certain sense of ownership; and clinging to it with more love and tenacity than ever, he speaks of it not as "The Gospel," but as "My Gospel." As Mr. Spurgeon says, Paul did not mean to indicate by this that he was the author of it, or that he had an exclusive monopoly of its blessings, but that he had so received it from Christ himself, and so fully taken it into himself, that he could not do less than call it "My Gospel." A very common phrase with Paul is "Our Gospel," which indicates that sense of preciousness which the true Christian feels as he revels in the richness and fulness of the promises of God in Christ.

But it is another suggestion from this unique phrase of Paul to which I wish to call your special attention. Whether Paul meant it so or not, I do not know. But whether he was conscious of it or not, there was a sense in which the Gospel was to Paul something different from what it was to anybody else. Not that Paul sought to make it a partizan gospel, but that it took on something of the color of his own individuality. We want to be very careful to keep ourselves free from partizanship or sectarianism, by which we would come to feel that we see the only truth there is in the Gospel. Truth is many-sided, and the Methodists see one side, the Presbyterians, and Baptists, and so on, see other phases of the truth, and it is not wise nor just that any one of us should claim to have the truth of the Gospel exclusively. Some day in heaven we shall see all around on all sides of truth, and then we shall lose all these distinctive names that are only local and temporary.

John Wesley once, in the visions of the night, found himself, as he thought, at the gates of hell. He knocked and asked who were within.

"Are there any Roman Catholics here?" he asked.

"Yes," was the answer, "a great many."

"Any Church of England men?"

"Yes, a great many."

"Any Independents?"

"Yes, a great many."

"Any Baptists?"

"Yes, a great many."

"Any Wesleyans here?"

"Yes, a great many."

Disappointed and dismayed, especially at the last reply, he turned his steps upward, and found himself at the gates of Paradise, and here he repeated the same questions.

"Any Wesleyans here?"

"No."

"Any Presbyterians?"

"No."

"Any Church of England men?"

"No."

"Any Roman Catholics?"

"No."

"Any Baptists?"

"No."

"Any Independents?"

"No."

"Whom have you here, then?" he asked in astonishment.

"We know nothing here," was the reply, "of any of those names you have mentioned. The only name of which we know anything here is 'Christian.' We are all Christians here; and of these we have a great multitude which no man can number, of all nations, and kindreds, and people, and tongues."

And so we must be careful that we live in harmony with the heavenly spirit while we are on our way thither.

And yet there is a sense in which Paul's gospel was peculiarly his own, and whenever we compare Paul's writings with those of John we see in each the temperament and peculiar characteristics of the individual man. And each in his own way presents the Gospel with a strength and a fervor and a beauty which are colored by his own originality. Not that either changed the Gospel of Christ from being what it was, Christ's Gospel, but each adorned and beautified the Gospel by the cultivation of the talents which God had given to him personally. And in that sense each of us may say with all reverence and yet with humble confidence, "My Gospel." And many who would never be won to Christ by Paul's gospel or by John's gospel may be won by the new setting which you are able to give the Gospel yourself. You can interpret the Gospel into the language and life of to-day so that your friend or your neighbor will be attracted by it when neither John nor Paul could interest him. It is certainly a solemn but at the same time a most inspiring thought that it is granted to each of us to present the one Gospel of Christ in a special edition of our own, illuminated through God's grace by our own personal consecration and fidelity in such a way that some will find Christ in it who would not be able to find him in any other gospel that ever was proclaimed. Let us be careful that our gospel gives no uncertain sound, and that we make it as attractive as the living presence of Christ in our hearts and the aid of the Holy Spirit can help us to do.

XXX.

MAKING THE MOST OF THINGS.

Luke ix. 10-17.

THIS incident of the loaves and fishes is in harmony with God's providence everywhere throughout all time. God is not stingy, but neither is he wasteful. There is abundance, but nothing is thrown away. The rain and the sunshine and the wind are made to work economically, so as to bring about the best results on all sides. At this feast which Christ produced from the five loaves and two fishes, there was such an abundance that no hungry man or woman in the crowd was tempted to stint in eating, and yet Christ was careful to have the fragments gathered up.

It seems to me that the great lesson is that the larger the worker the smaller the resources demanded. Five loaves and two fishes were entirely inadequate to feed the multitude if Peter had been host, but with Jesus at the head of the table they were more than sufficient. We often see this illustrated in common life. A little man requires large resources to accomplish anything. A large man with wide horizon, with immense capacity to work, can do great deeds with almost any weapon. A first-class carpenter can take two or three tools, and using each of them for a dozen purposes, can produce more satisfactory results than an indifferent workman with the whole tool-chest at his command.

I think it is a characteristic of great men and women that they make a great deal more of the work to be done than of the method of doing it, or the tools by which it is to be accomplished. See Gideon, with his three hundred men, each with his pitcher and the little lamp inside of it. The ingenuity of Gideon was worth tens of thousands of soldiers. To bring about the victory there was required either a large army, or three hundred men, each carrying his pitcher and lamp with Gideon to make the combination. The weapons did not amount to anything without Gideon, but with Gideon to combine them and handle them they were like the five loaves and two fishes in the hands of Jesus.

David in the camp of Saul, with Goliath brandishing his spear in the distance while the army of Israel trembled for fear, is another illustration of the same sort. A sling and a little smooth stone, such a thing as shepherd-boys play with, were very small and insignificant in themselves. But with a man like David, who had fought a bear single-handed and plucked a lamb unharmed from the teeth of a lion, and whose soul trembled not in the face of a giant, a shepherd's sling and a stone were not to be despised. David's weapons were very ordinary, but he brought very extraordinary courage and skill and experience to work with them. Better a thousand times have a shepherd's sling and a smooth stone with a David to handle them, than a Remington rifle with a coward behind it.

It is a great thing to acquire this art of making the very most of all the ability we have. There are many people who do not give anything to the support of the church because their income is small; but how great a mistake they make is indicated by Christ's pleasure in and praise of the woman who cast her two mites into the treasury. A very little money, if it is the measure of one's ability, and is given in the spirit of prayer and cheerful self-denial for Christ's sake, may be, through him, multiplied in its influence far beyond what we are able to conceive.

Many others have no special gift for public speech, and do not find it easy to express themselves concerning their own religious purposes, and hence they do not do anything in that way, and give the Lord no public confession. One could not make a greater blunder than that. For who of us has not heard the stammering words of the child or the timid Christian, spoken out of a warm heart of love, the influence of which to comfort and bless the Holy Spirit multiplied even while they spoke as marvelously as Christ enlarged the feeding capacity of the five loaves and the two fishes?

We ought to learn this lesson in our church work. We should bring all the ability we have into the common stock of resources to help on the kingdom of God in our church. If we can sing, we ought most cheerfully to bring it to swell the chorus of praise we offer to God in the public worship. But many have musical hearts who can not sing with their lips, and that power of appreciation and that ability to shed cheerfulness should not be held back from the Lord's treasury.

There are some people who make a great deal of their sorrows and failures, but who are always minifying their joys and resources for good. There is the same temptation in our church work to look on the critical side, and in that way we depress others and hinder rather than help courageous advancement. A little girl in Kansas has recently given the telegraph companies a vast amount of trouble in a peculiar way. Her daily duty was to herd a large drove of cattle on a range through which passed the telegraph lines. For weeks, some hours nearly every day, these lines absolutely failed to work, and the trouble seemed to be in the vicinity of where this girl herded her father's cattle; but it was a long time before they discovered the cause. Finally they found out that in order to get a better view of the herd the girl had driven railroad-spikes into a telegraph-pole, and whenever she got weary watching the cattle from the ground she would climb the pole and seat herself on a board across the wires and watch her herd from that lofty station. Whenever the board happened to be damp it destroyed the electric current and cut off all telegraphic communication between Denver and Kansas City. When discovered, and informed of the damage she was doing to the business of the telegraph lines, she was greatly surprised, as she was utterly ignorant of the fact that her seat on the wires interfered with the working of the lines.

I have many a time seen a few grumbling church members sit on the wires of spiritual life in a church until they seemed to shut off all heavenly communication. It does not take many such to spoil a prayer-meeting or lower the spiritual tone of any service. Surely it is not an enviable thing to go through life noted only for our ability to sit on the wires and keep the messages of joy and peace from coming to the hearts of tempted and tried men and women. Rather let us by our cheerfulness, our appreciation, and our spirit of thanksgiving make the very most of everything that is good and helpful, either in our own life or in the life of our church.

XXXI.

HOW NOT TO WANT EVERYTHING.

1 Thessalonians ii.

IT is easy enough to see what answer Paul would give to our question when we read this splendid paragraph in this love-letter of the great apostle to the Christians at Thessalonica. Paul's glory and joy was in winning conquests for Christ. As he expanded the kingdom of Jesus among men, his heart was filled with rejoicing. The matter of fame, or money, or of personal comfort, or luxury, became a very insignificant affair. It was a question of advancing the glory of Christ whom he loved with all his soul, and winning lost men and women to know the joys of this new salvation, in which he daily exulted. This great purpose had such a hold on Paul that it entirely freed him from any slavish anxiety concerning minor things. Paul got hungry like other men, he got cold and shivered like others, he liked his freedom, and to be chained to his guard was not pleasant to him more than to others; but none of these things had power to discourage him or give him any real sorrow, since he was able to bear witness for Christ and win souls to love his Lord in spite of dungeon and chain and hunger and cold.

Our lesson, then, is very simple. To liberate yourself from a great many little wants you must have one supreme want which is so much greater than all the others that in its satisfaction you shall have your glory and your joy. If you think mostly about yourself, and let your mind concentrate on your personal comfort, it is marvelous how your wants will multiply, and what a host of ghost-like anxieties and cares will spring up to disturb your peace.

Jerome K. Jerome, in his book, "Three Men in a Boat," gives a striking illustration of how easily people can get into trouble if they set about morbidly brooding over their own personal condition. He was in the British Museum one day, reading up the treatment of some slight ailment which he thought was like hay-fever. He got down the book, and read all he came to read; and then, in an unthinking moment, he idly turned the leaves and began indolently to study diseases generally. He came to typhoid fever, read the symptoms, and it was borne in upon him that he certainly had it. He sat for a while frozen with horror; and then in the listlessness of despair again turned over the pages. He turned to St. Vitus's dance; found, as he expected, that he had that too; began to get interested in his case and determined to sift it to the bottom. And so he started alphabetically, read up ague, and learned that he was sickening for it, and that the acute stage would commence in about two weeks. Cholera he had with severe complications; and diphtheria he seemed to have been born with. He plodded conscientiously through the twenty-six letters, and the only malady he could conclude that he certainly did not have was housemaid's knee.

We may laugh at that, but we do just as absurd things about the most important matters of life every day. Make the wants of your life paltry enough, and they will be thicker than the frogs in Egypt. Make the purpose of your soul large enough, and all the smaller things will fall into their insignificant place and cease to trouble you.

Mr. Spurgeon had once been into the country to preach, and when traveling back to London suddenly found that he had lost his railway ticket. A gentleman, the only other occupant of the compartment, noticing that he was fumbling about in his pockets, said, "I hope you have not lost anything, sir?" Mr. Spurgeon thanked him, and told him that it was his ticket that was missing, and that, by a remarkable coincidence, he had neither watch nor money with him. "But," Mr. Spurgeon added,

"I am not at all troubled, for I have been on my Master's business, and I am quite sure all will be well. I have had so many interpositions of divine providence, in small matters as well as great ones, that I feel as if, whatever happens to me, I am bound to fall on my feet, like the man on the Manx penny." The gentleman seemed interested, and said that no doubt it would be all right. When the ticket collector came to the compartment he touched his hat to Mr. Spurgeon's traveling companion, who simply said, "All right, William." Whereupon the man again saluted and retired. After he had gone, Mr. Spurgeon said to the gentleman, "It is very strange that the collector did not ask for my ticket." "No, Mr. Spurgeon," he replied, using his name for the first time, "it is only another illustration of what you told me about the providence of God watching over you even in little things; I am the general manager of this line, and it was, no doubt, divinely arranged that I should happen to be your companion just when I could be of service to you. I knew you were all right, and it has been a great pleasure to meet you under such happy circumstances."

If we are possessed by this supreme purpose to do the will of God, the circumstances which are around us will not be able to master us, but we shall influence our environment, just as a bed of roses pervades the air with its perfume. If we kick against the pricks of life, we shall wound ourselves every time; but if we press forward, with our eyes on the supreme prize, we shall not mind the scratches of every-day difficulty more than the hunter does the thorns that tear his coat, or even make the blood come, as he pushes through the thicket after the game.

If we confine our thoughts and expectation of happiness to the narrow round of this world's doing, we shall soon come to the end of our tether, like a horse that is staked out in the pasture, and the things we have will seem very small when compared to the things we want.

A young Swedish girl was very homesick. "You ought to be contented, and not fret for your old home, Ina," said her mistress, as she looked at the dim eyes of the girl. "You are earning good wages, your work is light, every one is kind to you, and you have plenty of friends here."

"Yas'm," said the girl; "but it is not the place where I do be that makes me vera homesick, it is the place where I don't be."

And isn't that a good description of the source of our discontent always? A supreme purpose to please God here and now, to do his will this present hour, a consciousness of his interested, smiling presence, will relieve us from the homesick longing and discontented hungering for the things we can not have at present. If we only knew how to fully appreciate the privileges we have every day in our fellowship with Christ, and in our opportunities to serve and praise God, most of the wants that fret us would cease to have any power to annoy.

I have been reading the story of a lovely old Christian man who had been a fine singer, but who came to be afflicted with a cancer on his tongue. He went to the hospital for an operation, and when all was ready he held up his hand and said: "Wait a bit, doctor; I have something to say to you." The operator waited, and the patient continued: "When this is over, doctor, will I ever sing again?"

The doctor could not speak; there was a big lump in his own throat. He simply shook his head, while the tears streamed down the poor fellow's face, and he trembled convulsively. The sick man then appealed to the doctor to lift him up, with which request the physician complied. He said: "I have had many a good time singing God's praises, and you tell me, doctor, I can never sing any more after this. I have one song to sing, which will be the last. It will be a song of **gratitude** and praise to God as well."

Then from the surgeon's table this ripe old

Christian sang one of Isaac Watts's hymns, familiar to many of us:

> "I'll praise my Maker while I've breath,
> And when my voice is lost in death,
>   Praise shall employ my nobler powers;
> My days of praise shall ne'er be past
> While life and thought and being last,
>   Or immortality endures."

Let us learn our lesson to-night—the lesson of liberty from small and petty slaveries through self-surrender to one lofty and glorious service.

XXXII.
EVERY-DAY LIFE MADE EASY.

Psalm xxxvii. 1-19.

It is very easy to see that, according to the Psalmist's idea, the way to bring peace and comfort into every-day life is to go forward courageously to meet its duties, with the assurance that God means kindly toward those who are doing right and are steadfastly doing his will. The only safety in this world is in courage. Cowardice is the greatest danger. Some people go mincing their way along, examining cautiously every step they are to take, as tho they thought God had hordes of wild Indians ambushed in the thickets along the path of life to suddenly swarm out and tomahawk them. Such an idea of God would be more true of the devil than of the perfect Father who is revealed to us in the Bible. If we go along the way of life feeling and acting as tho the whole world were against us, and that we have to pick out our own way and take care of ourselves, then we have a sure recipe for misery. When we get it into our hearts that it is not the devil's world, but God's world, and that he has not deserted it, but is still in it causing all things to "work together for good to them that love God," we can afford to go on without fretting because of "evil-doers." We can see wicked men prospering and good men passing through hours of trial, and yet know that the "all things" will work out their righteous result in the end. Some day we shall diligently seek after the wicked man who prospered for a time, and he will have disappeared; and we shall see the good man, who for a while was passing under the cloud, with his face shining like the sun, and the rainbow of God's promise spanning the cloud through which he has been safely led.

Another way to make every-day life easy is to keep the heart in tune with God's will. God always wants us to do right. We shall always have discord when we are conscious that we are doing wrong. But if we will simply ask what is right, and try to do that every day without any compromises in the matter, or any quibbling over it, we shall find that our hearts will sing a very pleasant tune. Nothing can ever seriously disturb us except the consciousness that we ourselves have done wrong. No storm of trouble can beat about us so fiercely that angels may not visit us in its midst, as they did Paul on shipboard, or Jesus in the garden of Gethsemane. No dungeon can be so dark that God's messengers will not find their way into it, and no prison walls are so solid but he can shake the doors open. In the midst of every trying experience, if the heart is at peace with God there will be sweet music there that will more than make up for any outside trials. Keep the heart right, and you are sure of melodies of happy meditation that will make the most toilsome day full of pleasant things. Some one sings:

> "There's a cricket within the Christian's heart,
>   And a pleasant song sings he;
> Let him sing of the mercy and love of God
>   That hourly falls on thee
> Let him whistle them out full loud and clear,
> And never be drowned in sorrow's tear,
> But all through the dark of trouble's night,
> Let him chirp and sing till the morning light!"

Another way to make every-day life easy is to be quick to make amends for any blunder into which we may have fallen. We are very human, and are as prone to make mistakes as the sparks are to fly upward. Some people's mistakes never seem to hurt them much, they repent of them and get out of them so quickly. I have seen a horse so nimble-footed that it would stick its foot into a badger-hole while going at full gallop and get out so quickly that it would not stumble, while another with less sense and agility would run its leg in up to the knee and turn a somersault, to the great risk not only of its own neck, but of its rider's. There are two kinds of people illustrated by this figure. Some people are like David, who was a man after God's own heart not because he never blundered, but because he was quick to repent and confess his sin and take a new tack. How many times when we find we have misjudged a friend, and through some misunderstanding have taken a wrong position, if we at once confess it we may make it all right, while if we go on stubbornly holding a wrong position because we do not like to seem changeable, we darken not only one, but many days. A German soldier, an ensign, made a blunder during some maneuvers of troops which were being inspected by Frederick the Great. That passionate king ran after him, stick in hand, that he might beat him. The ensign got away and jumped a ditch, leaving the king on the other side still brandishing his cudgel. The colonel of the regiment came up to the king and said: "Sir, the young ensign doubtless committed a blunder. I have just received his resignation from your majesty's service. I am sorry, for he was really a good soldier, but he can take no other step." The king said: "Send him to me." The ensign came, expecting to be beaten, or possibly sent to prison.

On his entering his presence the king said: "Here is your captaincy, sir, which I tried to give you this morning, but you ran away so quickly I could not catch you." How much better it was for the king to turn it that way than to stubbornly hold out in the wrong, and, besides doing an unjust and foolish act, lose a good soldier.

In addition to all these things, in order to make every-day life easy we shall every one of us have need of forbearance and patience. To restrain the quick word and hold it back so that it does not get said, will save many an uncomfortable half-hour. It may rankle in the heart for a minute, but if you set your teeth together and do not say it, the person who has vexed you, not knowing you wanted to say it, will not be hurt, and five minutes later you will thank God for your restraint. Most of us need to pray the prayer of the hymn:

> "Sweet Patience, come!
> Not from a low and earthly source—
> Waiting, till things shall have their course—
> Not as accepting present pain
> In hope of some hereafter gain—
> Not in a dull and sullen calm—
> But as a breath of heavenly balm
> Bidding my weary heart submit
> To bear whatever God sees fit;
> Sweet Patience, come!"

XXXIII.

THE SELECTION OF CLOTHING FOR THE SOUL.

Luke xv. 11-24.   Matthew xxii. 1-13.

I AM struck with the expression in this old parable of the prodigal son that it was "the best robe" that the father ordered to be brought out and put on his wayward son who had now come back home. The best is none too good for the sons of God. And God wants to clothe us with the very best. What do you think is the best? If you could look about you and clothe your life just as you pleased; if you could reach up on to the shelves of this great wardrobe of a world and pull down any garment you wished, what would you choose as your idea of the "best robe"? If you could just take one robe, which you were to wear all the way through, which one would you choose? Would you take money or would you take character? Money is a good thing and will surround one with a great many comforts, but it can not give peace. A man may have millions and yet not be able to buy resignation or contentment. Tears are just as bitter and sobs just as heartbreaking in a mansion as in a flat of three rooms. Every worldly garment, however rich, is doomed to decay from the first.

A story is told of Mrs. Horace Greeley, who had a strong antipathy to kid gloves, and never wore them upon any occasion. One day, it is said, she met Margaret Fuller on the street, and instead of greeting her with any usual salutation, she touched Margaret's hand with a shudder, exclaiming: "Skin of a beast! Skin of a beast!"

"Why, what do you mean?" asked Margaret in surprise. "What do you wear?"

"Silk," returned Mrs. Greeley,—"silk always."

Margaret touched her hand and shuddered, saying: "Entrails of a worm! Entrails of a worm!"

So it is that death and decay are written upon every earthly robe, and in the severest storms of life that come to us they will leave us unclothed.

Think of it, how many things there are that money can never buy. We want faithful friendship, we want pure, sweet love, we want happiness, and many a man has dug his way into a gold-mine trying to find them; but no earthly Klondike has a vein of those rich metals. And when death comes the monarch is not more independent than the farmer or the mechanic. His crown, his palace, his army are all nothing, and his power drops from his nerveless fingers as helplessly as does the poor man's little all. Money and power and fame are all fine things to have, but if one can have only one robe, he would be very unwise to choose any of these. It is very foolish to choose what we must leave behind at that critical hour when death shall open the gate upon our eternal career.

Surely there can be no doubt that a good character is the best robe there is in the whole universe of God. Dr. George H. Hepworth well says that it is better to be poor and noble than rich and miserable. It is better to be strong in your heart than in your purse. An upright man can walk through the darkness of the graveyard without fear or trembling. Just before we slumber at the last it will be happier to hear an angel's voice bidding us welcome to the skies than to be told that we shall die a millionaire. In the last analysis the only man of real worth, who is well clothed, is the man of good deeds and lofty faith. You can exaggerate the value of your bank account, but not the value of your trust in God.

Money is a good thing, but God is better. Let us work hardest for what is noblest. Not greed, but faith, will stand you in good stead by and by. Make your life sweet with good deeds and pure thoughts. Set your days to the music of righteousness. Be a whole man or a whole woman, true, loyal, brave, and wholesome. Such a life is clothed upon in youth or age, in prosperity or adversity. Whatever comes will seem to fit you if you trust God and are sure that his will is best.

Some one gave Billy Bray a suit of clothes, remarking as he handed him the parcel, "The Lord told a Christian friend to send you this suit, but I am afraid it will prove too large."

"Oh!" exclaimed Billy, "if the Lord sent it, it is sure to fit, for he has my exact measure."

The Lord has your measure and mine, and if we leave it to him, his providences will fit us perfectly. There is a very delicate touch in one of Paul's letters in which he says we must put on the Lord Jesus Christ. You will never have a cloak that will fit you so gracefully; you will never wear anything that will be so attractive, and you will never have a garment that will caress you so tenderly as when you have put on Jesus Christ.

I have been reading the story of some men who went hunting in the Northwest and shot a mother bear who was protecting three little cubs. The sun was getting low, so they skinned the bear and were starting off when one of the men said: "Those cubs will die soon without their mother."

"That's so," the others agreed, but none offered to care for the little ones. Then one of the men said: "Fred shot the mother, and he ought to take care of the babies."

"Well, I won't let them die," said the man mentioned; and soon the cubs were in a bag and slung over his back, and he started bravely homeward.

They were not a very pleasant load, and kicked and squirmed until he was tempted to throw them away.

When they got to camp the motherless pets were put in a box and given something to eat; but eat they would not and yelp they would, making a distressing noise. He took a switch and whipped them, but they only cried the louder. At first every one was sorry for them; but by and by, as the crying was continued, everybody began to scold on account of the noise.

"Kill them," it was finally urged.

Two or three times the young man who had brought them home went to them intending to take them out and kill them, but each time they would stop crying instantly and look so trustingly at him that he would go away and leave them. At last he grew hard-hearted, as no one could sleep with such a racket. He went up very bravely to the box, and called on one of the others to help him. But he refused.

"Do for mercy's sake tell me what to do, then! Say, I have an idea," he exclaimed, and he rushed

out and brought back—what do you think?—
why, the mother-bear skin! Covering this over
something, he put it in a corner of the box. The
men stepped back so that they could see without
being seen, and pretty soon each little cub had
smelled the mother-skin and had nestled up close
to it as contented as could be, and soon they were
sound asleep. Even those hardy hunters went
away with moist eyes to see them go so quickly to
sleep by their dead mother's skin.

We are orphans in this world, all of us, without
God. No one of us has ever snuggled down to
rest in perfect peace until we have felt close about
us the comforting folds of the divine love.

XXXIV.
THE SPIRITUAL CUPBOARD.

John vi. 1-40.

BREAD is the staff of life. Cakes and preserves and ice-cream are good enough in their place, but if any one of us had to choose a steady diet of just one thing we would not hesitate long before choosing bread. So the great staple of a Christian life is feeding upon Jesus Christ. We must get our motive, our spirit, our example, all from him. Only as we feed upon him shall we become strong and muscular Christians.

The healthy condition of the body depends largely upon the partaking of wholesome nourishment at regular intervals. One may have good food, and yet if he does not partake of it with sufficient regularity and frequency he will soon find his physical system demoralized. Let any man here try taking two square meals on Sunday and then fasting, with an occasional glass of water or a cooky, until Friday night, and he will be too weak to walk to prayer-meeting. And yet that is what some people do, practically, in a spiritual way. I fear that the old-fashioned family altar in every Christian home, with its reading of the Bible and spiritual song and prayer, has been done away with in a great many religious families. It can not be neglected without great spiritual loss; it furnishes an opportunity for taking spiritual food regularly every day. Don't imagine that you are too busy, and excuse yourself that way, for we really have no right to be too busy to feed our spiritual nature. One of the early Methodist preachers in Kentucky was stopping over-night at the house of one of his church members where a certain Judge Cone and his wife, from Nashville, Tenn., had also stopped to pass the night. When Mr. Bolton, the host, handed the Bible to the minister for family worship in the evening, he said to him in an undertone that he would best make the service short, as the judge was probably not accustomed to such things.

The old man said, "Very well, very well," but he looked pained. He read only two verses of Scripture and then knelt down. "O Lord," he prayed, "we are very poor and needy creatures, and we know thou art able and willing to supply all our wants; but Mr. Bolton says that Judge Cone and his wife from Nashville, who are with us, are not used to family worship, and however needy we are, there is no time to spare in telling thee our wants. Amen."

The judge was greatly taken aback, and so was his host. Between them they persuaded the faithful old preacher to continue his prayer, which he did with great earnestness and spiritual fervor.

The wise Christian will take time to eat the spiritual food which is necessary to build up the inner and by far the more important man.

It is idle to think that one may store up enough at one time to make up for days and weeks of spiritual starvation. Spiritual dyspepsia, if not so apparent, is far more common than its physical type of disease. Some people will go to a special service for a week or two and stuff themselves with highly wrought spiritual food, arousing the emotions, and then seem to feel that because they have overgorged the spiritual stomach they may excuse themselves from both food or service for the next month or two.

I have heard of a very stout woman who resolved to consult a physician about her corpulence. The doctor drew up a careful dietary for her. She was to eat dry toast, plain boiled beef, and a few other things of the same lean sort, and in a month return and report the result.

At the end of the time the woman came, and was

so stout she could hardly get through the door. The doctor was aghast.

"Did you eat what I told you?" he asked.

"Religiously," she answered.

His brow wrinkled in perplexity. Suddenly he had a flash of inspiration.

"Did you eat anything else?" he asked.

"Why, my ordinary meals!" said the woman.

Some people seem to have no more sense of propriety than that, concerning the spiritual cupboard.

The Sunday services and the prayer-meeting, with their sermons and exhortations and songs, are intended only to instruct us and inspire us, and teach us how we may feed upon Christ, the living bread that came down from heaven.

To be spiritually fed, we must daily meditate upon him. By Bible reading and prayer and special times of thought upon Jesus we must so feed upon him as to obtain spiritual nourishment. When Arnold was writing the life of Frederick W. Robertson, the saintly preacher of Brighton, he went one day into a bookseller's shop, and found that the proprietor had been used to attend on Robertson's ministry, and had in his possession a portrait. He said: "Do you see that picture? Whenever I am tempted to be mean I run into this back parlor and look at it; whenever I feel afraid of meeting a difficulty I come and look into his eyes, and they put new force into me." If a picture of Robertson in a bookseller's back room will do that for the bookseller, what may we not expect when we have the picture of Jesus Christ in our souls! Yea, more than that, when we have his spirit brooding over our spirit, feeding our inmost self, nourishing our fainting purpose, and strengthening us for every trial of life!

XXXV.
THE DUTY AND PRIVILEGE OF FORGIVING THOSE WHO INJURE US.

Matthew vi. 1-15. Ephesians iv. 22-32. Colossians iii. 8-17.

PERHAPS the superiority of Christianity to all worldly philosophy shines out clearer at this point of forgiveness of injuries than almost anywhere else. Cultivated, worldly people have the silver rule which enjoins that we shall treat other people as they treat us; but it is only Christianity which has the golden rule of love which requires us to do unto others as we would like to have them do unto us. Even the religion of Moses held to "an eye for an eye, and a tooth for a tooth." But Christ soars far higher into the realm of love and forgiveness. Christianity is high-water mark in human living. It is an extra height of goodness. Christ says that unless our righteousness shall exceed the righteousness of the scribes and Pharisees, we have no right to be called after his name. We must climb up out of the foggy atmosphere of holding grudges and wreaking vengeance, to bask in the sunshine which is reflected in the face of Jesus Christ.

But John told the truth when he said that the commandments of Christ are never grievous. This duty of forgiving those who injure us is not only not a heavy burden added to the weary load of life, but it is the only sure way to happiness.

It is the sure indication of a noble soul to overlook slights and refuse to revenge injuries. Sir Thomas Browne says: "Hath any wronged thee? Be bravely revenged. Slight it, and the work's begun; forgive it, 'tis finished. He is below himself that is not above an injury."

In the course of Gladstone's great speech on the second reading of the historic Home Rule Bill, he went out of his way to pay a graceful compliment to the son of Joseph Chamberlain, who had delivered his maiden speech in that debate. "The speech was one," said Gladstone, "that must have been dear and refreshing to a father's heart." The effect of these generous words on Chamberlain, who had of late lost no opportunity to affront the great Premier, was very marked. He covered his face with his hands while the tears ran down his cheeks for many minutes.

Many a silly enemy has been turned aside by the refusal of the one attacked to retaliate.

While Spurgeon was still a boy preacher, he was

warned about a certain virago and told that she intended to give him a tongue-lashing. "All right," he replied, "but that's a game that two can play." Not long after, as he passed her gate one morning, she assailed him with a flood of billingsgate. He smiled and said: "Yes, thank you, I am quite well; I hope you are the same." Then came another burst of vituperation, pitched in a yet higher key, to which he replied, still smiling: "Yes, it does look rather as if it might rain; I think I had better be getting on." "Bless the man!" she exclaimed, "he is as deaf as a post. What's the use of storming at him?" And so her railings ceased and were never again attempted.

There is no grace which more adorns human nature than the grace of forgiveness and mercy.

When the young Queen of the Netherlands recently visited Paris, the ladies of Paris were delighted with a necklace that she always wore, whatever might be her costume. This ornament consisted of a gold chain with a very original clasp, it being composed of a snake whose body partly encircled the neck and chain. The head of the snake was a single huge diamond, of wonderful fire and beauty, while the body of the reptile was composed of smaller diamonds, rubies, and other precious stones. But I know of a necklace more beautiful and enduring than that, and one which every one of us may wear. It is the one spoken of by Solomon when he says: "Let not mercy and truth forsake thee: bind them about thy neck."

The grace of forgiveness is not only ornamental, but it is a grace which can flourish only where there is warm personal fellowship with the heart of Christ. Did you ever see a watercress-pond in the midst of winter? It is a very attractive sight. With the thermometer far below the freezing-point, and with deep snow covering the ground and the branches of the trees, the patch of watercress stands out in striking contrast—a spot of vivid green like a carpet on the surface of the pond. That the plants are able to grow and flourish under such apparently impossible conditions of weather is due entirely to the warm springs which feed the pond. The water welling forth from the warm heart of the earth saves them from freezing. So the only way a generous, forgiving spirit can be always maintained in the midst of the freezing selfishness of the world is to have the fountain which Christ has promised—the fountain of living water—evermore springing up in the heart.

A forgiving spirit absorbs and takes out of our social fellowships many of the poisonous hurts that would otherwise cause sorrow. It is like a tamarack tree which, growing in a swamp, will absorb all the microbes of malaria and save the whole community from ague and fever. And so healthy is the tree itself that in purifying the water and atmosphere it seems to grow all the more vigorously and gracefully. No one ever lost in graciousness of spirit or beauty of soul or peace of heart by forgiving an injury.

God has so made the world that every such generous, Christlike deed shall have its influence not only now and here, but evermore and everywhere. In Gray's famous "Elegy" there is a line which bemoans the fate of flowers that waste their sweetness on the desert air. But modern scientists assure us that the poet was wrong in his conception, and that no flower ever yet thus wasted its sweetness. They explain to us that all the flowers in the world—whether they be the laurels and the rhododendrons of the lofty mountains and the deep forests, or the palms of India and Africa, or the gorgeous century plants of the American desert, or the roses of the valleys—are perpetually enriching the atmosphere and making the earth a healthier and sweeter place in which to live. Many of these great gardens of God grow and flourish hundreds of miles from any human habitation, but God causes the winds to catch up their fragrance, and the air is sweeter in Cleveland because there are flowers growing in South America and China.

The God who knows how to make the flower-perfume cross the oceans will not be at a loss to find a way to make your deed of forgiving love and mercy help the world, and that not only now, but centuries after you are rejoicing in heaven.

If we have such a spirit it will be doing good under all the circumstances of life which may come to us. Frederick Weatherby sings a song of "An Eolian Harp" which is a true song also of the Christian heart:

"I set my wind-harp in the wind,
   And the wind came out of the south;
Soft, soft, it blew with gentle coo,
   Like words from a maiden's mouth.
Then like the stir of angel's wings,
   It gently touched the trembling strings;
And oh! my harp gave back to me
   A wondrous, heavenly melody.

"I set my wind-harp in the wind,
   And a storm from the north blew loud,
From the icy north it hurried forth,
   And dark grew sea and cloud.
It whistled down the mountain's height,
   It smote the quivering chords with might;
But still my harp gave back to me
   Its tender, heavenly melody.

"Ah, me! that such a heart were mine,
   Responsive tuned and true

When all was glad, when all was shine,
  Or when storms of sorrow blew.
That so, 'mid all the fret and strife,
The jarring undertones of life,
My life might rise to God, and be
One long, harmonious symphony."

XXXVI.

COMMONPLACE HEROES.

1 Samuel xxx. 1-25.

THIS is one of the most interesting stories in the Bible. There is, perhaps, no other story which brings out in such bold relief so many characteristics of David. His grief on discovering the capture of his family brings him very close to us. We stand a little in awe of a man who can slay a giant with a sling and a smooth stone, and the majesty and the beauty of his psalms exalt him among the geniuses; but when he stands among his soldiers sobbing and crying for his wife and children carried away into captivity, we creep up close to him and lay our hands on his shoulder and sob with him in sympathy. The psalmist and the slayer of giants is forgotten; he is our brother.

But it is just like David to brush the tears from his eyes and prepare to go after the enemy and rescue his loved ones. David was a man of action. The great work of the world is done not so much by the giants and the geniuses as by the men of energy, who may weep for an hour like other men, but who are able to throw themselves into the saddle and gallop after the enemy for the other twenty-three hours in the day.

It is just like David, again, that even in his great hurry and anxiety he should have taken time for prayer, for David's salvation was in this, that at the bottom his soul was reverent toward God. David was always blundering; he could get into more mistakes and sins than most people; but there was no malicious purpose to sin in David's heart, and he was quick to repent and confess his wrong.

The success of David's undertaking was remarkable, and yet that, too, was characteristic. He had a habit of success; as have all men who make their faith and works go together. David never used prayer to take the place of what he could do himself. Some people seem to think of prayer as a makeshift to cover their own laziness. David wanted God's help; he knew he could not succeed without it; but he did not ask the Lord to succeed without David. Many a life which is getting to be a chronic failure would soon have the air of perpetual success if David's prayerfulness and energetic fighting qualities were both imitated.

The special theme, however, which I wish to emphasize is found in this last paragraph, which tells of David's treatment of the two hundred men who were so worn out that they were not able to go beyond the Besor, and who had been left there in camp to take care of the baggage. When the four hundred who had gone ahead with David had won their great victory and were coming back with the flocks and herds—not only their own, but those captured from the enemy—some selfish, greedy fellows among David's soldiers got up a scheme to cheat those who had been left in camp out of their share of the spoils. They said among themselves that they would not give to the men who stayed behind anything except to allow each man to have his wife and children. And they were going to send them back to their burned homes and ravaged fields without any part of the spoils that were taken from the enemy to indemnify them for their losses. David's solution of the matter reveals the secret of his great power as a leader over wild, half-tamed men, whom he was able not only to hold and control, but to inspire to the most heroic deeds. His words are courteous and gentle, but they are very firm. You feel the iron hand under the velvet glove. "Then said David, Ye shall not do so, my brethren, with that which the Lord has given us, who hath preserved us, and delivered the company that came against us into our hand. For who will hearken unto you in this matter?

but as his part is that goeth down to the battle, so shall his part be that tarrieth by the stuff: they shall part alike." This decision commended itself so thoroughly to David and to the people that it came to be a part of the common law of the land. Nothing David ever did reveals more perfectly his character as a statesman.

No doubt many of the bravest men David had were among those footsore and faint men who were compelled, to their own mortification and sorrow, to camp beside the Besor. In remaining in camp, taking care of the stuff, they had fulfilled their duty under a good deal harder circumstances than did those who went on to battle. This is of interest to every one of us. There is not a man or woman among us who does not remember some tiresome, tedious day when we lay with sore feet and sorer heart watching over the stuff beside the Besor. It requires more heroism many times to keep cheerful and patient when all we can do is to lie by, than it would to go out and fight for the cause that is dear to us.

Many a mother who has abilities for conspicuous social or public service has been chained for years by her fireside, standing by the stuff in the care of her little children; but God has not overlooked her heroism, and has seen to it and will see to it that she has her share of the spoils. Susannah Wesley was one of the very best educated women of her time, and it is doubtful if any woman of that day had greater abilities; and yet she could do nothing but simply stand by the stuff, and toil day and night for that great family of nineteen children. But John Wesley's sermons and Charles Wesley's hymns and millions of Methodist adherents throughout the world render their tribute of spoil to Susannah Wesley.

No doubt some of you are at this moment chained in a narrow place to a little round of commonplace duties, while your soul looks longingly to the wider horizon and to the better opportunity to exert and express yourself. But let us remember that while we may be forced to lie in camp for a time, God is not footsore or weary, but will ride on to victory. He will take our will and purpose and longing for the deed we are not able to do, and will divide us our share of the spoils.

The oft-quoted line, "They also serve who only stand and wait," is realized in every day of ordinary life. God's soldiers are not all on tented field. The great majority of them are in the fortresses of home and social and business life, where they stand with quiet courage to hold the battle-line against ignorance and sin. My old Oregon friend, Joaquin Miller, sings a song of this sort of battle:

"Nay, not for fame, but for the right;
　To make this fair world fairer still.
Or lordly lily of a night,
　Or sun-topped tower of a hill,
Or high or low, or near or far,
　Or dull or keen, or bright or dim,
Or blade of grass, or brightest star—
　All, all are but the same to Him.

"Oh, pity of the strife for place;
　Oh, pity of the strife for power;
How scarred, how marred, a mountain's face;
　How fair the fair face of a flower!
The blade of grass beneath your feet,
　The bravest sword; aye, braver far
To do and die in mute defeat,
　Thou bravest conqueror of war.

"When I am dead say this, but this—
　He grasped at no man's blade or shield,
Or banner bore, but helmetless,
　Alone, unknown, he held the field;
He held the field with saber drawn,
　Where God had set him in the fight;
He held the field, fought on and on,
　And so fell fighting for the right."

XXXVII.
THE ODD SPARROW.

Matthew x. 24-31. Luke xii. 6-7. Psalm lxxxiv.

GOD cares for little things. He is as careful about the painting of a tiny moss-blossom as he is about the splendid rhododendron. He has made delicate little insects of which you could hold ten thousand in the palm of your hand as carefully and as perfectly as he has formed the human body. Neither does he forget his creatures after they are made. He who has great choruses of angels, and in whose ears the morning stars sing anthems, does not despise the little bird's song. He is not more thoughtful about the eagle which flies in the face of the sun than he is about the dainty sparrow. Where a sparrow has built her nest and reared her brood and sung her song of thanksgiving was in David's thought one of the altars of God. Think of it—a bird's-nest temple! A tiny cathedral of green leaves where a sparrow's chirping incense goes up to God! Is your nest so true a temple as that? How abundantly God has dealt with you! In what full measure he has given you blessings! What are you giving back in return? Is your heart a place of worship? Is your home one of the altars of God?

There is nothing sweeter to a human heart than the thought that God cares about us, and that it is impossible for us to be lost in the crowd so that we are forgotten of him. If any of you feel as David did once when he said, "My days are consumed like smoke; . . . my heart is smitten, and withered like grass; . . . I am like a pelican of the wilderness: I am like an owl of the desert; I watch, and am as a sparrow alone upon the housetop,"—you may still have the comfort that even the sparrow alone upon the housetop is not forgotten of God, but is tenderly cared for by him. Happy will it be for us when we can obey the injunction to cast our care on him and let it rest there.

Many of us are as foolish as a poor immigrant who was discovered walking on the tracks of the Lehigh Valley Railroad in New Jersey. On his back he carried a huge package containing household utensils as well as clothes. He seemed tired, tho he trudged sturdily on. He had not, however, acquired the veteran tramp's skill in walking on the ties, and his journey was evidently telling on his physical powers more than the same distance by the roadway would have done. An agent stopped him and ordered him off the track, telling him that he was liable to arrest for trespass, besides incurring the risk of being killed by a train.

The man, who was a Hungarian, demurred, and produced a railroad ticket, good from Jersey City to Scranton, Pa. The agent looked at him in amazement, and asked him why he was walking when he might ride. The Hungarian replied that he thought the ticket gave him only the privilege of walking over the road. His right was explained to him, and the tired man delightedly boarded the first train that stopped.

Don't you think the angels are just as much amazed at you, to see you trudging along, footsore and anxious and careworn, when if you used your tickets of divine promise you might " mount up on wings as eagles "? If we really trust God we may all sing:

> "Care thou for me! Let me not care!
> Too weak am I, dear Lord, to bear
>   The heavy burdens of the day;
>   And oft I walk with craven feet
>   Upon life's rough and toilsome way;
>   How sweet to feel, how passing sweet,
> Thy watchful presence everywhere!
> Care thou for me! Let me not care!
>
> "Care thou for me! Why should I care,
> And looks of gloomy sadness wear,
>   And fret because I can not see
>   (Thy wisdom doth ordain it so)

> The path thou hast marked out for me?
> My Father's plan is best, I know.
> It will be light, sometime—somewhere—
> Care thou for me! Why should I care?
>
> "Care thou for me! Let me not care!
> This, each new day, shall be my prayer;
> Thou who canst read mine inmost heart
> Dost know I am exceeding frail;
> Both just and merciful thou art,
> Whose loving-kindness ne'er shall fail;
> My human nature thou wilt spare.
> Care thou for me! I will not care!"

It is a very pretty touch, I think, in Luke's account of the Savior's words, where he said, "Are not five sparrows sold for two farthings?" We know from Matthew's story that the ordinary price of sparrows in the market was two for a farthing; but it seems that on market days they sold five sparrows for two farthings—that is, they threw in an odd sparrow. That is Christ's idea of God's infinite care, for he says, "Not one of them is forgotten before God;" and again he says that not one of these little sparrows falls to the ground without his notice. How kind it is of our heavenly Father to give us these illustrations in such a way as to comfort the most fearful! When he would express to us the characteristics of his thoughtfulness he does not use for an illustration his care over the eagle, or the nightingale, or the swan—splendid and fashionable birds, with mighty wing or rich plumage or beautiful song; but of the raven, an ugly bird of ill omen, or a little helpless, chirping sparrow. This he does to indicate to us that tho we are sinful and disheartened enough to be compared to a raven, or lonely and little enough to be compared to a sparrow—even an odd sparrow without a mate—yet he is watching over us with the tenderest love. Surely in that confidence we may sing to our hearts the song which Paul Fleming sang to himself:

> "Let nothing make thee sad or fretful,
>   Or too regretful:
>   Be still.
> What God hath ordered must be right;
> Then find in it thine own delight,
>   My will.
>
> "Why shouldst thou fill to-day with sorrow
>   About to-morrow,
>   My heart?
> One watches all with care most true;
> Doubt not that he will give thee, too,
>   Thy part.
>
> "Only be stedfast, never waver,
>   Nor seek earth's favor,
>   But rest.
> Thou knowest that God's will must be
> For all his creatures, so for thee,
>   The best."

XXXVIII.
THE MOUNTAIN OF THE GIANTS.

Joshua xiv. 12.

CALEB is one of the heroes of the Old Testament who is without a spot on his record. He was one of the spies sent by Moses into the Promised Land when the children of Israel made their first approach to Canaan. When they returned with their report, Caleb and Joshua alone of the twelve urged Moses to go at once into the Promised Land and possess it. The other ten, however, had been very badly scared by the giants whom they had seen. They declared that these men were so large that they felt like grasshoppers in their sight, and that they lived in such walled cities that it would be the height of folly for Moses to lead his army against them. Caleb was then comparatively a young man, only forty years old, full of courage, full of faith in God, and he did everything in his power to change this cowardly verdict, but was unable to do so.

We come back to him now forty-five years later.

He is eighty-five years old—or rather, as Oliver Wendell Holmes would put it, "eighty-five years young." There never was a man whom that change of phrase would suit more perfectly than Caleb. He declares to Joshua that he feels as young as ever in his life, and that he is as vigorous as in his early manhood. We can not improve on his own language about it, which he utters to Joshua when he comes to him on his birthday, and asks for a birthday present in the shape of a chance to carry on a campaign against the mountain strongholds of the giants that had so completely scared out his fellow spies a generation before when he was young. He says: "Lo, I am this day fourscore and five years old. As yet I am as strong this day as I was in the day that Moses sent me: as my strength was then, even so is my strength now, for war, both to go out and to come in. Now therefore give me this mountain, whereof the Lord spake in that day; for thou heardest in that day how the Anakims were there, and that the cities were great and fenced: if so be the Lord will be with me, then I shall be able to drive them out, as the Lord said."

We have revealed here the kind of metal of which this old man was made. His enthusiasm, his courage, his faith and hope—all the things that make a man strong and brave, powerful to conceive, endure, and accomplish—were as alive and real in him as ever. The truth is that conscious fellowship with God keeps men young and fresh in their vitality and enthusiasm. A worldly, material life, given up to purely earthly pursuits, loses its freshness and zest very early. Nothing is more pitiful than to see middle-aged men and women, and others scarcely so old, out of whom all the fresh impulse of life has disappeared — people who are *blasé*, and who have *ennui*, who have seen everything, and heard everything, and done everything that is worth doing, according to their idea; for whom life has lost its appetite and its interest. Such people are more worthless than if they were dead. If only they were dead, somebody might occupy the place where they are; but living, they clutter up the world as old rubbish of furniture no longer used clutters up a house.

But it is impossible for a man to keep fresh and joyous and hopeful into old age, ready to do daring things when other men are making their wills, if he have no source of hope, no reservoir of courage, higher than this world of time and sense. The horizon is too narrow, the sky is not high enough, to give breathing-space or to furnish visions that exalt the soul. But men who take long views of life like Caleb, men who have faith in God, who are conscious of God's pleasure in them, who serve him day by day, and who, while they fight their own battles, know that they are fighting also the battles of the Lord, who do common duties in a lofty spirit—these are the men to whom life never gets dull or monotonous. If you want to go on through life with the glow of perpetual youth on your soul and the ardor of eternal hope stirring your heart, then you must let the great thoughts, the great purposes, of the eternal God fill your soul and lift you up into the realm of those things that live forever. If you cling to the clods you will die with the clods; if you aspire to the stars you will rise to them forevermore.

There is something very inspiring in the picture of this noble man on his eighty-fifth birthday asking for himself not a chance to retire on his laurels, or some easy place where he may rest from his labors and enjoy his honors, but begging to be given the very hardest field there was in all Canaan, that he might do exploits. He might easily have asked—what certainly would not have been denied—for some choice territory that had already been captured, where he would have had no enemies to fight. But that is never the spirit of the hero. Instead of asking for an easy job, Caleb asked Joshua to give him the mountain of the giants. He does not ask Joshua to capture it for him and then make him a present of it. There are plenty of people who could do that. All he asks is an opportunity to go and capture it for himself. He is not unaware of what he has to contend against. He knows the men are giants, that they live in walled cities on mountain summits; but Caleb says: "If so be the Lord will be with me, then I shall be able to drive them out." God honored the old man's faith and gave him great victory, and a great inheritance for his family and his people.

We ought to get a personal lesson out of this. In the building up of our character we should not be hunting for easy things to do or for easy things to be, but seek for the highest and the noblest achievements of human endeavor. There is always a temptation with us to make our life easy at the expense of making it little and narrow. Great things are never easy. You can fell a single tree across a brook and go over on it, but to throw the Brooklyn bridge across the gulf between Manhattan and Long Island is hard; yet is it not worth the difference? So in personal character it is always easier to live a compromising sort of life that bends to the standards of the half-wicked world in which we live, to give way to the unchristian prejudices that prevail in our social set, to fall in with the gossipy, semi-slanderous tone of conversation, to let greed have its way in business—easier to do as others do than to stand out strong and faithful for the thing that is right, for the standard of Jesus Christ. But the greater life pays, nevertheless, in the long run. Men may sneer at the time, and say that the man with the larger views of honor and righteousness is a fanatic and a crank; but he gets his inning in God's good time.

When "Chinese" Gordon led the regular troops of China against the famous Taiping rebels, he won the great admiration and regard of the Chinese government. Toward the end of that war he accepted the swords of four rebel leaders whose lives were promised by Gordon because their surrender doubtless saved many scores or hundreds of loyal Chinese soldiers. After the surrender the government violated the pledge he had given, and against his stern protest executed the rebel leaders. Gordon in disgust tore up his commission, returned his Chinese decorations, sent back a special gift of fifty thousand dollars he had received from the grateful Emperor, and scornfully refused to have further to do with a ruler who did not observe solemn treaties. It would seem that Gordon might have become supreme in China over all except the Emperor, yet he set all aside for the sake of teaching a valuable world-lesson which is quoted in all nations until this hour.

These thoughts are not appropriate for geniuses

only, but for every man and woman among us. It is false to ourselves to seek less than the very holiest, strongest life which we may lead. We are the sons and daughters of God. We are the brothers and sisters of Jesus Christ. We are fellow heirs with men like Abraham, and Joseph, and David, and Elijah, and Daniel, and Isaiah, and Paul. No height of nobility to which men ever climb, no lofty heroism by which men were ever inspired, no beauty of holiness that has ever adorned human character is beyond our reach. All things are possible to us through Jesus Christ our Savior.

XXXIX.

THE SPECIAL VALUE OF AVERAGE PEOPLE.

Matthew xxv. 14-23. Luke xix. 12-19.

WE never hear very much of this man with two talents. There are a great many sermons and exhortations devoted to the man with five talents, and perhaps more yet to that selfish and idle fellow who had only one share and hid it in order to escape the responsibility of its use. But these middle men with their average capital have slipped through so far without very much notice in the commentaries or among the sermon-makers. And yet I think we ought to be most interested in the man with the two portions, for if I mistake not he is about our size. I don't think there are many geniuses among us who have gone to the limit in our shares of intellectual stock, and I don't think there are very many who have been given only one share. The people who fill the congregations, both men and women, are mostly those who have their average two sharse of common stock in the concerns of life.

Now the thing that I want to impress on your minds is that he is a very fortunate and ought to be a very happy and useful man. I know it sounds a little like an echo when he goes up and makes his report: "Thou deliveredst unto me two talents: behold, I have gained two other talents beside them." And I can imagine him feeling a little ashamed to have to make the same report as the man who had five talents except that his was smaller because his capital was smaller. And yet, if you will notice, he gets fully as much appreciation from his master as the other man who had doubled his five shares. The welcome which he receives is just as hearty as it was in the case of the genius.

The man who has only average ability and average opportunity for his work is always in danger of underrating himself and of being tempted to say: "If I could do something large and splendid, something worth doing, I would do it gladly; but there will be hundreds of others who can do the same thing, and I'll seem just like an echo of somebody else, or a small edition of some rich and influential man that goes ahead of me." And so he is tempted to throw up the fight and not do anything because he can not do something out of the ordinary. There could be no greater mistake than that. The overwhelming mass of the necessary work of the world is done by people who have only this average ability and opportunity. Once in a while there is a great ranch like some of those in California or Minnesota, on which some one man gathers a hundred thousand bushels of wheat a year; or a great mill like those in Minneapolis, where flour goes out at the rate of thousands of barrels a week; but the world is fed mostly from little farms where only a few acres of wheat are planted, and from the smaller mills that turn out a few barrels of flour a day. In the great manufactories it is necessary to have some men with a genius for leadership to superintend departments and to carry on business, but the great work is done by the men with only two talents, who stand in their special place and do the one item of work for which they have fitted themselves. When war comes, generals and colonels and captains are necessary, and are usually very abundant on paper, but they get wonderfully thinned out when the battle is on, and a half-dozen names only stand out after a campaign; the great burden of war falls on the two-talented men down in the heart of the great war-vessels, who feed the fire with coal and look after the steam; or who load the guns; or who on land, in ordinary uniform without shoulder-straps or other rank than the common private soldier, face death with heroic fortitude, and die rather than desert their flag in the presence of the foe.

A man like Gladstone is a great gift to Great Britain, but the ordinary "Tommy Atkins," of whom Kipling sings, is the real two-talented backbone of English power in the world. Bismarck was the genius of Germany, and a giant personality, but your ordinary German soldier-citizen, with his black bread in his knapsack, is the two-talented German force that gives power to the Prussian name. In the church it is the same, among preachers as well as among laymen. There is now and then a genius in sermon-making, in ecclesiastical organization, or in evangelistic service; but the great work of the church is done by men of only average ability, who, with steady, faithful devotion to God and man, do duty so persistently that the coming of their feet upon the mountains is beautiful because of the gracious spirit with which they carry their good tidings.

In the ordinary work of the church this fact is equally as marked. Most churches have more major-generals than are needed; but there is always a demand for the people who are willing to help in whatever is at hand—who will pray at a moment's notice, or bear a brief, loving testimony of God's goodness without feeling that it is necessary to exhort or tell a long story; the people who will visit the sick, or pass around invitations to attend church among the neighbors, or call on a family just moved in and invite them to church, or go two blocks out of the way every Sunday morning to bring a child to Sunday-school, or teach a Sunday-school class, or any one of twenty other things constantly needed in the progress of a live, active church. Their abilities are not so large but that they can adapt themselves to the needs of common folks. They are not afraid to shake hands with people as if they liked them and were really glad to see them. They are not too fashionable or esthetic to laugh out loud when they are glad, or to shed tears without being ashamed in the presence of real grief.

These average folks make good fathers and mothers. They are not above telling Bible stories to their children in the old-fashioned way; not too well dressed to go and kneel down and pray with them by their cribs at night; not too cold and dignified to go and talk with a poor sinner and persuade him to seek Christ, or kneel by his side at the altar with an arm about his neck, and love and pray him into the kingdom.

These average folks can afford to be cheerful. They are not geniuses, or fashionable swells, or great society leaders, with a reputation and a dignity to take care of; they are just good, whole-souled, human folks who have common sense and big hearts, who love God and love his people, and do not blush when they say so. God give us more of them!

XL.
CHRIST'S PHILOSOPHY OF COMFORT.

John xiv. 1-27.

THE world is sick at heart with sorrow and trouble. Religion is medicine for the soul. Jesus Christ said he was a physician. He came to comfort the sorrows of humanity. I want to lay the emphasis on that verse in this wonderful chapter in which the Master says, "I will not leave you comfortless." That is a great declaration. No mere human being could ever deliberately and honestly make such a promise as that. Many of us love our friends so tenderly and devotedly that we would never leave them comfortless if we could help it; we would gladly suffer any loss for their sake; life itself would seem a light risk if it might shelter them and protect them from sorrow. But the human arm is so weak, and the limitations of our human power are so imperative, that the most heartbreaking thing about life is that we can not always bring comfort to our dear ones in trouble. Lord Rosebery, ex-Prime Minister of England, son-in-law of Rothschild, who has known what it is to have unlimited wealth at command, says that the greatest pleasure that comes from wealth is the possibility it gives the possessor, through change of climate and luxurious surroundings and medical skill, to prolong the life of loved ones. And yet Lord Rosebery has worn crape for many years because wealth beyond measure and the gentlest climates of earth and the best medical skill known in the world could not save his beloved from the grave.

But Jesus Christ says with all confidence, "I will not leave you comfortless." He will not leave us comfortless in our sins. Tho our sins be as dark and ungrateful as Peter's when he denied his Lord in the hour of his greatest emergency and swore he never knew him, and thereby was plunged into the darkest despair; tho our sins be as black as that, if we repent as did Peter the loving Christ will not leave us comfortless. The very first message that he sent to the disciples by the angel after his resurrection had in it a special comforting sentence for Peter. So if your heart is sore on account of your backsliding, and your penitent spirit turns toward him, you may hear Christ saying to you as tenderly as to the disciples of old, "I will not leave you comfortless."

He will not leave us comfortless in the fears and

worries of life. Do you remember the night after the day when he fed the thousands of people with the five loaves and the two fishes?—when he went up alone into the mountain to pray, while the disciples went out in their boat on the lake? The storm came up in the night, and it seemed certain that they would be wrecked. In the midst of the storm Jesus, who had been near by watching it all, tho they did not know it, came walking to them on the waves. When they saw him they knew it looked like him, but they were frightened and thought it must be his ghost. But Jesus called out to them, "It is I; be not afraid!" He was not willing to leave them comfortless. Are you in the midst of the storm? Does life seem dark and uncertain? He is the same Christ as then. He loves you as tenderly as he loved that little boat-load of disciples. Open your heart to him in your sorrow, in your fears, and he will not leave you comfortless.

He will not leave us comfortless when life draws near its close. We shall not grow old alone; we shall not go alone into the valley of shadows. We shall not confront the grim ferryman without a companion. How tenderly Christ assures us on this point. "Let not your heart be troubled: ye believe in God, believe also in me. In my Father's house are many mansions: if it were not so, I would have told you. I go to prepare a place for you. And if I go and prepare a place for you, I will come again, and receive you unto myself; that where I am, there ye may be also." The whole philosophy of Christ's comfort lies in the power of personal love. See how Christ explains the comfort he will bring: "I will not leave you comfortless: I will come to you." The secret of it all is there. We shall not be comfortless, because we shall have Jesus. We shall find him in our Bible; we shall find him when we pray; we shall walk with him when we carry his burden and wear his yoke; we shall come in touch with him when we minister to his brothers and sisters; he will sit at the table of our hearts, and we shall have communion with him day by day.

Nothing can separate us from this love of Christ. So long as we stand faithful to him there is no power in all the universe strong enough to break that fellowship of love. We may pillow our heads upon his promise not to leave us comfortless, for he has at once the strength, the wisdom, and the love to carry out his promises. And when at last our call comes to go forth into the eternal world, it will be the same Christ whom we have known here who will meet us there, and with whom we shall dwell forever.

XLI.
HOW TO MAKE THE BIBLE A PERSONAL BOOK.

Hebrews i. Psalm xlii.

WE lose, I think, the very best of the Bible unless we approach it in a spirit of spiritual hunger and alert readiness to find its message as sent to our own hearts. The loss of individuality is never greater than in the study of God's Word. God has made no two of us alike; even the outer world is a little different to each of us than it is to any one else. Each sees his own beautiful pictures in the spring-time forest, in the glory of the evening clouds, and the splendor of the sunrise on the mountains. So it is in our appreciation of men and women, and in the fellowship and blessings which we receive from them. Who of us does not know some great, strong, generous-natured man or woman who is a different personality to every one of a dozen friends? He is a genuine, honest friend to every one of them. His friendship is full of delight and comfort and blessing to each one. He is perfectly natural in each case, and yet how different he is in his attitude toward them. One touches him on the side of art; another enjoys with him a literary fellowship; one is interested with him in political ideas; to another it is outdoor sport and adventure which awakes their talk; another communes with him about the problems of social life between men and women in this complex and baffling age in which we live; another has touched the fountain of his affection, and they look deep into each other's eyes and know the love that passeth knowledge; while still another enters into the heart's temple, and they burn incense together before the altar of their God in spiritual fellowship. How little you have said about this man when you have said that he is the friend of all these men and women! He is not only the friend of all, but the friend of each, and the friend of each in a different way. He is the friend of each one as he needs; each gets from him the comfort and inspiration and friendship that he asks.

Now that is the way God deals with us. With him is infinite resource, and the Bible is the revelation of his heart to us. In it there is a message for every mood, for every experience, for every longing of the soul—a message for the sad and the weary, a message for the glad and the strong, a message for the deep, probing thinker, a message for the courageous and daring worker. And if each one will come to the Book with his own honest longing and let his hunger have full play, the Bible will give him the food he needs.

The trouble is that many people rarely if ever come to the Bible at first hand. They read what this man or that man says about the Bible, until, if they do come at all to read it themselves, the mind and the heart are confused with the half-dozen spectacles of other men's thoughts through which they have been looking. They come to the study of the Bible dependent upon other people, and without that aroused and independent spirit of research which every one of us must have to get from the Bible the peculiar message which it holds for us alone.

I think the worst thing the Roman Catholic institution has done for the world has been the robbing of such multitudes of souls of ever knowing the Bible as a personal book. A brilliant Roman Catholic priest of Paris, who has left that communion because of the new light which has come to him, has been making an address in which he says some very striking things. Among other statements he makes is this: "A French Christian is a man who dares to read the Scriptures for himself and with his own eyes. The Roman Church, when it puts the Bible into the hands of its priests and its people, first puts a bandage over their eyes; or rather, instead of a bandage, it puts on them blue or green spectacles so that they see blue instead of white, and green for black. And it says to them, 'If you, unfortunately, read with your own eyes, you will be damned!'" Now Abbé Philippot, who makes this utterance, has come to the conclusion that God has a personal message for each soul, hence he bursts out with the exclamation: "Does not God dwell in France as much as in Italy? Is not the sun over our heads? Does not God make the corn to grow in France? The Pope is no more in communication with heaven than we are. Or has the Vatican perhaps a special telegraph-wire from the throne of God to the Pope's chair? If the Eternal will condescend to speak to the Pope, we will humbly ask him to speak to us too."

This French brother has got at the root of the matter. But is it not true that there are thousands of Protestants who never come to the Bible except with blue or green spectacles on? The reason is, we do not read it enough. We do not sufficiently cultivate the habit of going to it for guidance when we are perplexed, or for encouragement when we are sad, or for the proper expression of our gladness when we are joyous. We can only make the Bible a personal book by translating it into our own lives and writing our own lives between the lines on the holy page.

Mark Guy Pearse tells the story of a fisherman who was converted in his old age. He was not able to read, and therefore had to do his own thinking, and so he pondered a great deal upon the Word of God which he had read to him. A friend visiting him one day, knowing how he loved the Bible, said to him, "Now, John, shall I read you a chapter?"

"Yes, if you please; I should so much like to hear a chapter. I do dearly love to hear the Word read."

"And what part shall I read to you?"

"About the Lizard Lights, please. Do read about them, for when I see them I always think I am near my heavenly home. I have often been out on the Atlantic on dark, stormy nights, and when I caught sight of the Lizard Lights I knew I was near Falmouth harbor and would soon be safely moored."

"I am afraid," ventured his friend, "that I do not know about the Lizard Lights."

"Not know about them! Well, I thought you were a gentleman, and had Scripture knowledge; but if you don't know about the Lizard Lights you must wait until Mary comes in."

A short time after, Mary, who was his daughter, came in, and the old man said: "Mary, where is that in the book about the Lizard Lights? You know you were reading about them last Sunday night."

"O father," she said, "that was not the Lizard Lights—it was the Israelites!" The old man had made a mistake of the head, but he had made no mistake of the heart. He had not apprehended clearly in detail, but the application was all right. The story of the Israelites told of the guidance of God in their wanderings, and the Lizard Lights had been the beacon which many a time had guided him safe into the harbor.

If we will come to the Bible with its fulness of incident, its stories of human life and of God's dealings with it, as tho it were God's message for us, we shall find that its pillar of cloud by day and its pillar of fire by night, its angel songs and its angel ministries, will all live again and glorify our own lives.

XLII.
JUICY CHRISTIANS.
Psalm civ.

DAVID declares that the trees of the Lord are full of sap. God is a good provider. He looks after his household well. If he makes a desert anywhere it is for a purpose: that there may be somewhere else fertility and fruitfulness that would not be possible without some furnace in which to warm the winds to caress olive groves and orange orchards. The Lord teaches his trees in the forest how to get the sap they need out of the earth and the air. He teaches each one individually how to find the particular juices necessary to sustain its life, to clothe it with beauty and nourish its fruit. The oak finds the right kind of juices to make acorns; the lemon the peculiar acid for its fruit. The peach and the pear and all the ten thousand other trees find in the earth and the atmosphere their own individual answer to their needs. Each one of them is full of sap.

Now the God who has been kind to the trees is not less kind to men and women. He means that we, too, shall abound in the sweet juices of the Christian life. If we go stunted and starved and fruitless, it is our own fault. This is a world of abundance. Nothing is eked out in a stingy way. The sunshine is never measured with a gas-meter nor the showers by the cupful. God is prodigal in flooding the world with sunshine and pouring out the riches of the clouds; he gives abundantly. And so Jesus Christ tells us that he came that we might have life, and have it more abundantly.

The Christian life is the most abundant life in the world. Nothing could be more lacking in truth than the statement sometimes put forth that the Christian life is narrow and mean and hard. As Dr. Watkinson well says, it is an utter misrepresentation to say that we are not free to enjoy al the opulence and beauty and delight of God's world. We are not thrust into a corner; we are circling in a sky. We do not paddle in a pool; we sail on a sea. All the pipes of nature are in our organ; all the strings of nature and society and intelligence are in our hearts. The true, sincere Christian has the most abundant life in the world. All things belong to us, and I think we ought to always make it clear. John Bunyan, clear-eyed as he was, turned a woman out of his congregation because she wore a silk dress. John Wesley declared that he dared no more write in an ornate style than he dare wear a fine coat. Michelangelo painted only sacred subjects. Frances Ridley Havergal would sing only religious tunes. But in these days I think we are compelled to look with suspicion on all that sort of thing. If people propose to narrow life down they must be able to give us a good reason for doing so; for, in the first instance, "All things are ours, things present and things to come;" and it is a mistake for us in any wise to impoverish our lives. Paul declares to Timothy that God "giveth us richly all things to enjoy."

A juicy Christian must be, in the very nature of things, one whose life is vital with the graces which were dominant in Christ. What were the peculiar juices of Christ's life? First of all, he was interested in people; he was never too bored to look into a case of oppression or to look after the needs of one who was sick or in trouble. His conversation and appearance were juicy with real tender human interest in the circumstances of the people whom he met. Let us cultivate an interest in people in order that we may thus bless them.

Christ's life was juicy with kindness. Was there ever a man who had such a genius for kindness? Just go back over his life—the dinners he attended, the fishing parties of which he was a member, the funerals where he was present, all his association with people, rich or poor, in happiness or sorrow —and how ready and alert was the kindness of Jesus to show itself in just the right way and promptly at the right moment.

The character of Jesus was juicy with reverent love toward God. People who got acquainted with Jesus not only felt the touch of his sympathetic interest, and became grateful for his kindness to them, but he inspired them with the conviction that his interest and kindness had a clear and definite relation to his own fellowship with God. He made men feel that they were his brothers because God in heaven was the Father of them all. He not only made people love him, but he made them love and glorify God.

Now I wish every one of us could have these three juices of the Christian life. There are others that I might speak of, but I would to God we might have these three: First, a sympathetic interest in our fellow men—an interest that will make us care whether they are out of work or not; whether they are having a good time or not; whether they are discouraged or not. Second, a prevailing spirit of kindness toward others, so that in any emergency that may come on us we may be depended upon to do the kind thing. We may not always be wise, we shall carry with us some of the blunders of the head; but the very juice of life may be such that no one who knows us will ever doubt that the heart atmosphere in which we live is kind. And then, finally, a reverent attitude toward God, so that the people who know us will know that we love God; that we live prayerfully and tenderly toward him, with a childlike feeling of love and confidence. With this understanding, I hope and pray that the recording angel, looking down on the men and women of this church, shall write, "The trees of the Lord are full of sap."

XLIII.
SLEEPY CHRISTIANS AND THEIR GENTLE LORD.

Matthew xxvi. 17-46.

No picture in the life of Jesus is at once so full of dramatic interest, of pathos, and of tenderness as this picture of the hours in Gethsemane. The last supper with its loving conversation has passed, and Jesus goes out into the garden with these loved disciples to endure the last great temptation and struggle of soul before his trial. Knowing that his strength must come from God, that in communion with the Father was his supreme refuge, there was yet within him a great longing for human companionship that brings him very close to us. He was going aside alone to pray, and yet he liked to feel that the disciples were near at hand, so that if he wished he could speak to them, or step back in a moment and find them watchful and loving.

Who of us does not know what that means? We face a trial that we must go through alone. We do not expect any one else to bear our burden, we know that only our own shoulders must carry it; but, oh! what blessed comfort to feel that some one cares, that dear hearts love us, and would carry our burden if they could, and are watchful and alert with their sympathy and their love; ready to put the pillow of their tender solicitude under our head; ready to sustain us with their words of good cheer and assurance of interest and fellowship in our sorrow.

But the shadow of the great sorrow was on these disciples. Of their friendship for Jesus there can be no doubt. Peter's sudden failure later that night by no means proves that they were not loyalhearted men. Many a soldier has run in a panic who afterward lived and died with unshrinking fidelity, as did Peter himself. But the strain of anxiety and the nervous tension of the hour, the unfathomable mystery of the situation, the weariness of the body, the influence of the supper—all these things combined to bring upon them a seemingly uncontrollable drowsiness, and so when the Master came back to them he found them asleep. They started up guiltily at his step, and with tender protest he said to Peter, "What, could ye not watch with me one hour?" And then not wishing to pain them unnecessarily, and looking as he always did for the good that is in everybody, he takes into account their weariness and their weakness, and says to them in comfort for their shame, "The spirit indeed is willing, but the flesh is weak." Again he came back, desiring to talk with them and find comfort in them; but they were sound asleep. This time he did not wake them, but softly, quietly, went back again to prayer. There were those who did not sleep—the heavenly Father listened to his conversation, the watching angels hovered near, longing to bring him support. Coming to them the third time, as they roused themselves he said, "Sleep on now and take your rest."

I have not selected this theme to make apologies or find excuses for any real negligence of Jesus on our part, but I have selected it rather that we may have the blessed comfort of knowing and feeling how infinitely tender and gentle our Lord is with our weakness. We may be always sure that Jesus does not misunderstand us. We are not always certain about that with our earthly friends; even the dearest and most faithful of them may sometimes feel that we could do better than we do. But when we do our best for Jesus he knows all about it; there is no danger of misunderstanding there. There is surely great comfort in that. No matter how weak and frail we are, Christ thoroughly appreciates it, and he will be infinitely gentle and tender with us if we do our best.

But, some one says, I have not done my best. I have been weak and halting. There has been many a time I might have kept awake and alert in Christ's cause if I had not weakly and wickedly gone into temptation. But even to you I bring the comfort of Christ's gentleness and forbearance, and urge you not to spend any more time looking back over the failures of the past; not to longer grieve the heart of your gentle Lord by useless personal upbraiding, but rather to obey him now, and to press forward by his help to a better life in the days to come. Nothing could be more foolish than to brood so much over the failures of the past that you lose hope for the future.

Mark Guy Pearse tells this parable: Once upon a time there was a man walking in the highway, and he fell down. No doubt it was partly his own carelessness. He, however, persisted that it was an accident. But the trouble was, that when he was down he stayed there, and spent all his time in telling everybody who would listen how it happened. Some shook their heads doubtfully, and that made him angry. Some sympathized with him, and that made him sad. At last there came a man who asked, "How long have you been here?" It was ten, twelve, fifteen years or more. The stranger shook his head: "I am sorry, very sorry."

"Yes," said he who was down, "it is a terrible thing to tumble down."

"That may be," said the man; "but there's one thing a thousand times worse."

"What is that?"

"Why, not getting up again."

I give that message to any discouraged one who has fallen by the way. Your failure is not that you have fallen, but that you do not get up. David was a man after God's own heart because when he had sinned and saw his wrong he repented of it promptly, and began again. "Go thou and do likewise." David said the gentleness of God made him great. Surely the gentleness of Jesus should inspire us.

XLIV.

THE POWER OF PERSONAL INFLUENCE.

Romans xiv.

NOTHING is more subtle and at the same time more powerful than our personal influence. I don't mean the influence we have upon others by the direct use of our reasoning powers in persuading them to do things, or by the exercise of some official prerogative which gives us power over the lives of others. I mean rather the influence of our example and spirit—the silent, unconscious influence which we are exercising on our fellow men and women about us all the time.

When I was a boy in Oregon we lived on a high hill, up in the foothills of the Coast Range Mountains. The situation seemed as healthful as could have been selected within a thousand miles. The water we drank came from a great spring nearly as cold as ice that plunged out from the hillside from some deep hidden reservoir in the mountain. And yet we began to have the chills and fever every summer-time. About the time the wind got settled round into the north the ague would begin to loosen our joints and make our teeth chatter, and life would become a burden. We were a long time finding out what was the matter. But finally we took into consideration the fact that a big beaver-dam lay off to the north of us, two or three miles away, and in the hot summer this water became stagnant and foul and covered with a green slime— a perfect hot-bed for the production of ague-germs. The north wind came along and picked up these invisible plagues and brought them over to us on the hillside. Now some people in their personal influence are like that beaver-swamp. Their lives are stagnant and unwholesome. There rise from them, in the very spirit of their lives, the germs of deadly moral disease. They do not need to do bad things purposely in order to have a harmful influence; this evil miasm rises from them, and, without their knowing it, there is carried from them to others a blight worse than any ague.

On the other hand, there are those whose lives are so fresh and strong, whose characters are so sweet and pure, that no one can live in the same neighborhood with them without receiving a breath as from the sea, refreshing and full of vigor and courage. You can not meet such people without being cheered and inspired. Your half-defeated faith and hope get nerve again in the sunshine of their strong, wholesome natures.

What we need to feel is, that whatever we really are, in our inner selves, we shall, in a greater or less degree, radiate to others in unconscious influence every day. If a man is honest, straightforward, and genuine to the core, he makes it easier for other people to be honest, and all sorts of insincerity seem horrible in his presence. But if a man is leading a sham, superficial, insincere life, it can not be otherwise than that the influence going out from such a character and career will be deteriorating; others will feel the blight of the insincerity, tho they can not prove it.

There is only one way to always have a good influence on people, and that is to be good ourselves. The unconscious influence comes most not from what you intend, but from what you really are yourself. Not what you do, but what you are— from that rises the influence that is to bless or curse. The great salt sea does not need to do things—only to rock and roll in its bed, and let the wind blow over it and carry away the wholesome medicine that brings vigor and health to the invalid. So if we are true to God and live reverent, cheerful lives, full of the atmosphere of faith and love and hope, it will be impossible for discouraged men and women to catch a whiff from off the salt meadows of our lives and not be the stronger and the better for it. Thus shall we fulfil the prophecy of Jesus Christ our Savior when he said, "Ye are the salt of the earth."

XLV.
THE LIVING BREAD.

John vi. 22-58.

MANY indeed are the illustrations which Christ uses to make us know his tender and loving interest in our salvation. He is called the Physician who is not looking after the well but the sick. He is the Good Shepherd who lays down his life for the sheep. He is the Vine which does not hold back the nourishing sap of life that he may revel in it himself, but pours it out with generous love into the branches, which consist of every one who loves him. He is the Way in which we may walk in safety, and feel sure that the foundation is solid beneath our feet. He is the Son of man in whom manhood blossoms in perfect flower, and we may not only breathe his fragrance, but hope through his grace and mercy to become like him. He is the Light of the world, shining into the darkest place, and if we follow him we have his word for it that we shall not walk in darkness. He is the Lamb of God who gave himself as a sacrifice in our behalf.

He is the Friend of sinners who seeks after the lost with patience and long-suffering kindness. He is the Brightness of the Father's glory, bringing heaven's beauty and splendor down to us, and showing us in his life among men the glory of God in our own human body. He is the Captain of our salvation, and did not hesitate to perfect himself through suffering. He is the Door, and no power on earth or in hell can hold us back from that Door save our own will. He is the Firstfruits of the great Easter truth, with the promise that every one who lives and dies in his precious faith shall be brought up from the grave to be with him in glory. He is the Bridegroom, and every soul that forsakes its sin becomes espoused to the Lord Jesus, and with a bridegroom's tender love he watches over us and longs for our marriage to him in heaven. And so I might go on through eighty titles that are given in the Bible to make known the majesty, the glory, the kindness, the long-suffering love of Jesus Christ toward us; and yet among them all there surely is no title more satisfying, more comforting to our hope and faith, than this assurance in the language of Jesus himself, that he is the Living Bread which came down from heaven, and that if any man eat of this bread he shall live forever.

What more can Christ say to us than he has said

in this vivid illustration? He has given himself to be our food. Our hungry hearts may feast upon him day by day. Christ brings to us in his teaching about God and man, about heaven and hell, about the immortality of the soul, concerning the forgiveness of sin, and the communion with God, and the comfort of the Holy Spirit—just those truths which we need to feed on every day as regularly as we eat bread. Many things we do not eat at every meal. The vegetables change with the season. Fruits and berries we have for a little while and enjoy them very much, but would tire of them if we had to have the same all the time. So it is with all the delicacies of the table. But bread represents the standby, the staple nourishment of life—something we feed on at every meal without weariness. Other things come and go, but by bread we live. So Christ is the Bread of Life.

There is something wrong with the spiritual appetite when we no longer enjoy feeding on the great truths which Christ gives us. It is always a sure sign of backsliding at heart when we do not enjoy sermons or books or conversation or music that bring Christ prominently before us. Who of us that are Christians can not remember times of special spiritual enthusiasm and enjoyment, when to attend the house of worship, where Christ and his suffering and his intercession were the chief themes, was to us the most joyous service in the world? At such times just to be alone and think about Christ, and commune with him in quiet, secret meditation, was to find a heavenly abiding-place in him. The prayer-meetings and the testimony-meetings, where earnest, warm-hearted Christians poured out their hearts' deepest longings and desires before the mercy-seat, and where grateful men and women gave testimony to the gladness of their Christian experience and their joyful outlook for the future, were places of constant inspiration. While our own hearts were in such a frame, preaching about Christ and about the great fundamental truths that he came to bring to us was the most delicious food to our souls. Now if all this is changed, and you find yourself caring little for the Bible, losing your interest in the old spiritual hymns, longing to go anywhere else rather than to the house of prayer, caring for other conversation far more than communion with Christ or knowledge of the advancement of his cause, then you may know that there is something the matter with your appetite. The trouble is not with the bread. It is living bread. It never gets stale; it is as delicious to the taste of a hungry spiritual nature now as it was in the days when Jesus fed the people here on earth with his own hand.

The loaves of spiritual comfort and blessing which Christ gives are of a kind that are as necessary now as they were eighteen hundred years ago. And they satisfy just as well. Men feed on them in hours of loss and misfortune, and their hearts are made strong; the sick and weak find in them the strength they need; the pilgrims in the valley and shadow of death find perfect content in feeding on this bread. Childhood, youth, middle life, and old age, whether dwelling in a tent or a cottage, in an attic or a palace, find in Jesus Christ the bread that came down from heaven. It will do to live by and to die by; and as Daniel and the Hebrew children had faces more healthy and beautiful than any of their companions who drank the wines and ate the meats of the court, so sincere Christians who feed upon the Bread of Life have countenances so hopeful and glad that they are a constant testimony to the goodness of God and the sufficiency of the Savior who gives them his own self upon which to feed.

XLVI.
HOW TO GET RID OF FEAR.

Luke xii. 1-40.

I DO not mean the kind of fear suggested by the Psalmist where he says, "The fear of the Lord is the beginning of wisdom;" that sort of filial fear is rather a mingling of reverence and love than fear in the modern sense of the word. I mean rather the fear which John has in his mind when he says, "Fear hath torment." All sorts of fear which has the power to torment us are unnecessary to us in a normal healthy and right condition. There is something wrong with us physically, mentally, or morally when we are tormented with fear.

I think we may find the secret of how to get rid of our fear of this kind in John's other declaration, "Perfect love casteth out fear." As I understand it, tormenting fear is always born of a sense of insecurity of some kind. If we do not trust our friends, we fear they will betray us. If we trust them perfectly, we have no fear. If we are not sure of the roof over our head, we fear it will leak.

How to Get Rid of Fear.

If we have doubts about our acceptance with God and the forgiveness of our sins, we have fears of condemnation. And so you may run up and down the whole scale of the human piano concerning all the dangers possible to a human life, and there is peace or there is torment just in proportion to the feeling of insecurity or security which we have in our own consciousness.

It is interesting to note the places in the New Testament where we are exhorted not to fear. For instance, we are urged by Christ to have no fear of our enemies who hate us because of our love for him. We are rather, he says, to take it as an indication that we belong to him and are sharing the fate of our Lord, which is proper. As Christ came off triumphant in spite of all his enemies, so if we share with him he will bring us off more than conquerors.

We are not to fear in sickness. When Christ went to heal the daughter of the ruler, he said to the father, "Fear not: believe only, and she shall be made whole." I do not mean by this that Christ will always heal our sick ones in the same way, but I mean that there is no cause for fear if they are in his hands, for either here or in heaven they shall be recovered from all their suffering and their sorrow, and his will is the best thing that can come to them or to us. We are not to fear because we are frail, or weak, or poor, and feel that we have no power to protect ourselves. Nothing could be more comforting than Christ's words on this point. "Are not five sparrows," says he, "sold for two farthings, and not one of them is forgotten before God? But even the very hairs of your head are all numbered. Fear not therefore, ye are of more value than many sparrows." Or again, "Consider the ravens: for they neither sow nor reap; which neither have storehouse nor barn; and God feedeth them: how much more are ye better than the fowls?" Or still again, "Consider the lilies how they grow: they toil not, they spin not; and yet I say unto you, that Solomon in all his glory was not arrayed like one of these. If then God so clothe the grass, which is to-day in the field, and to-morrow is cast into the oven; how much more will he clothe you?" Surely we ought to be comforted with these words.

It seems very clear that the only reason we have tormenting fear is either because we are not doing right, or because we do not trust God. In either case the way to get rid of our fear is to remove the conditions which cause it. We may depend upon it that so long as our consciences condemn us for doing wrong, we shall be harassed by fear; and we ought to be. It is not an indication of God's enmity, but sure proof of his love, that he has made the path of wrongdoing a haunted and fearful path. Only in consciousness of right is it possible to have fear cast out.

But if we have been going in the wrong way, Christ is willing to take us by the hand and lead us into the path of peace. Paul was on the way to Damascus warring against God when the great vision came to him that changed his whole life; and as soon as he bowed his heart to Jesus, Jesus was ready with words of good cheer to say, "Fear not, Paul." And he will be ready with the same cheerfulness to give us the same good cheer the moment we put ourselves in the right attitude toward him.

But if we are trying to do right and are still troubled with doubts of God's ability and willingness to care for us, how shall we get rid of tormenting fear from that source? The reading of God's promises, talking with Christian people who have lost their own fear, and conversing with the Lord daily in prayer, are great sources of cheer and comfort. I am sure if we avail ourselves of such help we shall soon think of the trials that come to us in a different way. A little girl had been told of hobgoblins that lurk in shadows and catch naughty children, and such foolish things, until she was afraid to be left in the dark at night. She was nearly crazed with tormenting fear. She came to live with a wise aunt who undertook to comfort the child by giving her a sweet faith in the care of God. She told her that darkness was only a blanket with which God covered up the world; how the flowers blanketed themselves in perfume; how little birds tucked their heads under their wings, and sat up in trees, each birdie by himself in his own little private room of twigs and green leaves, which the good God made so that the birds might have nice little dark homes to sleep in. She would fold the little girl into her crib and say: "The darkness is just like a great soft blanket that God sends to wrap the earth up in so it can go to sleep." Once, as the light went down rather suddenly, Maisie asked tremblingly: "Is a big black bear in the corner?" "Why, no, dear!" The light flashed up instantly so Maisie could see; then went down softly, and auntie said: "Dear, God is in the room—our good God." After a while Maisie learned to love the darkness. She called it "God's blanket." So we may be sure that if we are doing right, seeking to please God by our words and thoughts and conduct day by day, the trials of life, which seem sometimes so hard for us because we do not understand or do not trust him, are God's soft, warm blankets by which he is protecting us. If we love him perfectly, keep our confidence in him, all tormenting fear shall be cast out.

XLVII.

THE TAMING OF THE GREATEST SHREW IN THE WORLD.

James iii.

THAT is a very strong statement which St. James makes, "If any man offend not in word, the same is a perfect man." He goes on to explain a little by assuring us that a man who is able to control his tongue and completely master that nervous little member is able to bridle the whole body. The argument which he makes and the illustrations which he uses are all very strong and graphic. I think no one can turn away from reading this chapter without agreeing with me that the tongue is undoubtedly the greatest shrew in the world, and that the taming of the tongue is the mightiest work to which Jesus Christ has set himself.

One of the greatest lessons we have to learn in the school of Christ, when seeking to come into mastery of the tongue, is the value of holding our tongue, on many occasions, and not saying anything. We are told that a wise philosopher of ancient times bound his scholars to silence for five years, that they might not use their tongues till they knew how to govern them, nor speak until they had something to say. It is said that a young man once went to Socrates to learn oratory. On being introduced to the philosopher, he talked so incessantly that Socrates asked for double fees. "Why charge me double?" asked the young fellow. "Because," replied the orator, "I must teach you two sciences: the one how to hold your tongue, and the other how to speak." It is often harder to teach a man how to keep still in the proper place than it is to teach him to speak prudently when he breaks silence.

These illustrations that St. James uses are very searching. He compares certain kinds of words to fire. It takes but a very little spark from a match to start a fire in dry tinder, but when once it is started, and the wind catches it and begins to fan it, who can tell where it will stop? So the fire of an unkind word, or a jealous word, or a slanderous word, which starts up gossip or bids suspicion or hate lurk and smolder in the chamber of the heart, when once the winds of the imagination begin to fan the flames, may spread through a family or indeed a whole community, charring and blackening and destroying the peace and quiet and faith, it may be, of hundreds or thousands of people. Such a result often comes from a single malicious sentence spoken spitefully and perhaps afterward forgotten by the one who started it. Like the man who lights his camp-fire in the woods, and goes away carelessly, leaving the smoldering log to set the great forest on fire behind him, to burn down or blight ten thousand giant trees, so the baleful fire from a reckless sentence goes smoldering on until, fanned into venomous flame, it despoils and blights far beyond the thought or purpose of the reckless tongue that started it. A little word of temptation, tempting another to do what his conscience rebukes him for, is like the Roman soldier's torch flung into the holiest of all, which burned the sacred temple to the ground in the days of Titus—it burns down the whole temple of a fair young life.

St. James is not the only man in the Bible who warns of the danger of a tongue unbridled and uncontrolled. Job calls the tongue "a scourge," or a whip, by which severe wounds are made on the character, and which leaves its great purple welts on the lacerated peace and reputation. Jeremiah says the tongue is like "an arrow, shot out." David compares the tongue to a "sharp sword." St. Paul, speaking of the lips through which the tongue speaks, says of people of unclean conversation that "the poison of asps is under their lips."

Paul must have had the same thought in his mind that stirred St. James when he said that the tongue is "full of deadly poison."

Christ is the only one who can tame the tongue. He does it by cleansing the heart. When that poor demon-possessed man of Gadara had the devils cast out of him, he needed no more taming. No man had been able to tame him before, but when the evil spirits were gone he came to his right mind, and went away to glorify God among all the people who knew him.

In order to have "the soft answer" that "turneth away wrath," we must have the gentleness of heart which will make us quick to forgive and slow to wrath. Perhaps no one knows how much good he may do in this world by turning away the wrath and strife of others on occasion by gentle and tactful conversation.

The habit of restraint in speech was admirably illustrated by Lord Palmerston at the cutlers' feast in Sheffield, at the time of the great struggle between the North and the South in the United States. A noted politician who was present had made a violent speech, urging England to side with the South. It was Lord Palmerston's place to reply, and a word from him might have kindled the flames of war. He arose, and every eye was fixed on him. What he said, however, was merely, "I beg to propose a toast—The Ladies!" The fire died out, and the reaction was toward peace. Almost every day one has an opportunity with a few words to either fan strife into a flame, or quell it, by the tactful use of gentle Christian speech. Let us put our tongues into the hands of the great Tamer. If we do so, He will incite us to kind words that will awake a train of gentle influence which will tell everywhere for peace and comfort.

XLVIII.

THE DIVINE SIDE OF A REVIVAL.

Isaiah lxi.

REVIVALS of religion are in perfect harmony with the divine conduct of this world. God works by means of fresh impulse. The marvelous chemistry of nature is carried forward on that plan. There is life in root and trunk and branch, in field and forest, all the year round; but at least once a year a fresh impulse is given to nature, and the hillsides spring forth with a new green, the forests are clothed with a fresh baptism of hopefulness and courage, and the old oak, gnarled and twisted with the storms of five hundred winters, renews its youth. Every springtime is God's revival by which he keeps the old earth young and prosperous, happy and progressive.

Men grow in their intellectual and moral lives because they receive, every now and then, fresh impulses which inspire them to still greater exertion. There is not one of us who can not remember times when we had fallen into a rut, and life seemed monotonous and commonplace, and had lost its zest and appetite; when, from within or without, there came some experience, pleasant or bitter, which stirred our nature to its profoundest depths, and life became new, fresh, and vital. Every thoughtful man and woman can go back over their lives and count the great soul-crises when these new impulses came to them.

I have said these things to emphasize the fact that a revival of religion is not something unnatural and artificial. It is in God's order that ever and anon the religious life which has been working its way in our hearts, has been plowing and sowing, growing and yielding harvest, should have a renewal, a springtime revival of its enthusiastic gladness, that will fit it for still greater results. The religious life which has no such experience as this certainly fails in the highest enjoyment of the Christian religion.

Now just as surely as it is the divine graciousness that is manifested in the green grass in the pastures, the clothed forests of April, the orchard bloom of May, so just as surely it is the divine graciousness, the presence of the Holy Spirit in human hearts, which gives the beauty and the rapture and the saving power to a revival of religion. In both cases this heavenly presence comes from the infinite mercy and love of God. Unconsciously the earth prays to God; the frozen soil, the discouraged roots, the buried seeds, the barren branches of the trees, the desolate shrubs, cry out in their very need to the God who has light and warmth and wisdom to touch all these fruitless things into leaf and flower and perfume. Our needs also pray to God, and arouse his longing to bring blessing to us, and he is ever seeking to do so; but he has made us so much higher than the plants and shrubs—made us so like himself in the power of choice and in the sovereignty of will— that he waits, as does a father for the appeal of childhood, to bestow upon us the fulness of his blessing. If we open our hearts to God, and wait upon him, the divine power will clothe us about as a garment. All human effort is vain without this supernatural anointing; but that will not fail if there be the proper attitude of soul on our part.

It is this divine presence which we must expect, and depend upon, to give power to sermon, testimony, music, and word of exhortation. God has not deserted his world. He has not ceased to be interested in the souls of men. He was not more faithful to Elijah on Mount Carmel when he answered by fire than he will be to us. He is the same God who breathed upon the valley of dry bones in Ezekiel's vision, and caused a living army of invincible power to stand forth. He is the same

God who came as a mighty rushing wind on the day of Pentecost, and enabled a hundred and twenty, in a single day, to win three thousand converts to the cross of Christ. He is as willing to bless our preaching and pleading and persuasion as he was Elijah's or Ezekiel's or Peter's. He loves the sinners in Cleveland with as deep a tenderness as that felt toward any men or women who have ever lived. Let us open our hearts! Let us surrender our lives to be filled and mastered by the Spirit of the living God!

This divine presence came to the early disciples when they were of one accord in one place. The Spirit of God has ever required a harmony of spirit on the part of the friends of Christ as a condition of the doing of mighty works in the salvation of souls. It is not enough that the preacher wants a revival; there must be such a unanimity on the part of the church that the minister will feel sustained, as Peter must have felt on the day of Pentecost. In early Methodist days the people responded in amens and hallelujahs, very much as the Salvation Army does now; and it can not be denied that there is in this an element of power. I do not plead for the vocal amen or the outspoken hallelujah. What I plead for is the same spirit—watchful, alert, yielding itself in harmony to the pleading of the minister, and prayerfully sustaining the message which is being given to the people. My friend, the Rev. Albert J. Hough, has voiced this longing of every preacher whose heart is on fire to save souls in a little poem called "The 'Amen Corner.'" He says that—

> "In the planning of modern churches,
>   The service of Sabbath days,
> We have left out the 'amen corner,'
>   And smothered the soul of praise.
> There are faces that shine like Stephen's
>   When he saw his Master stand,
> With a look of love and welcome,
>   In glory, at God's right hand.
> There are eyes that answer divinely,
>   And hearts that in sympathy beat
> With all that is grand and holy;
>   But the service is incomplete.
> When the light of the Lamb comes filling
>   Faith's rapt and adoring ken,
> We listen in vain for the 'Glory!'
>   And the seraph-souled 'Amen!'
>
> "In the golden days when our fathers
>   The enemy put to rout,
> All the saints in the 'amen corner'
>   Pursued him with a shout,
> While the burdened hearts of the seekers
>   For pardon and perfect peace,
> In a flood of their 'Hallelujahs!'
>   Obtained a swift release;
> And oft when the preacher, in battle,
>   Seemed overborne by his foes,

The Divine Side of a Revival.

From the praying souls in the corner
  A mighty ' Amen ' arose ;
And it broke the spell of the tempter ;
  The heaven ceased to frown ;
Faith rose to the throne triumphant,
  And the glory of God came down.

" When the saints in the ' amen corner '
  Bowed, listening, on their knees,
They would hear the sound of a going
  In the tops of the mulberry trees ;
And, bestirring themselves in spirit,
  They moved with their heavenly host,
Stepped out on the promises boldly,
  And prayed in the Holy Ghost,
Till the flame of a grand revival
  Swept through the land abroad,
For the saints in the ' amen corner '
  Kept pace with the march of God.

" We have men in the pulpit filled
  With the wine of the kingdom new ;
There's the life of the grand old Gospel
  Still flourishing in the pew ;
We are singing the songs our fathers
  Sang in the days of old ;
We are telling the wondrous story
  Their lips so sweetly told ;
And the Lord with his church is dwelling
  In power as he did then ;
But the spell of silence is on her,
  And she needs the grand ' Amen.'

A Year's Prayer=Meeting Talks.

We are bearing suppressed emotion,
   Like fire shut in our bones;
Our only relief is in sighing,
   And in timid undertones.
Reestablish the 'amen corner,'
   The freedom of ancient days,
And the pent-up streams of emotion
   Shall flood the land with praise.

"When the voice of rejoicing nature
   The land with its music fills,
Not the least in the strange enchantment
   Is the echoing of the hills;
For the Lord of the whole creation,
   Who speaks in a thousand ways,
Is surrounded with 'amen corners'
   That answer his voice with praise;
And when I ascend, at his bidding,
   To that upper temple fair,
I will fly to the 'amen corner,'
   For I know he has one there."

XLIX.
THE HUMAN SIDE OF A REVIVAL.

John i.

WHEN we begin to talk about the human side of a revival the subject gets to be very personal; it strikes us right where we live. Let us not try to thrust it aside, but face our duty frankly and earnestly. I believe that all the members of this church are more or less desirous of a great revival of spiritual interest which will increase the spiritual delight and comfort of Christians, and result in persuading a great many who have been indifferent and sinful to seek and find Jesus Christ as their personal Savior. Let us ask ourselves the pertinent question, What can I do to bring about this revival, and to enlarge and spread abroad the tide of its influence?

First, you can think about it every day. There is a great deal in that. Put up the revival calendar, with its topics of sermons and its references to texts, where you can not help but see it frequently;

take it down on opportunity and study it with Bible in hand; think of the subjects that will be most likely to interest persons of your acquaintance, and, marking another calendar, hand it or send it to them. If you can not do the latter, you can at least do the first. Meditate on the reading every day. It will be with you as it was with the psalmist: while you muse the fire will burn.

Talk about it every day; give the weather a rest. Say nothing about your cold or your rheumatism, and check like dissertations on the part of your friends by some hopeful talk about the revival meetings. Nothing can withstand a flood of conversation about a subject of real interest. If you can get a thousand people talking about a single thing, you can stir up a great city. Make up your mind that you will talk about the revival meetings through the month of January more than about anything else.

Pray about it every day; this will be easy for you if you are thinking about it and talking about it. What we think and talk most about very naturally comes uppermost in our minds when we begin to talk with God. Determine on a quiet place and time each day when, whether you feel like it or not, you will go and pray to God for his blessing on the pastor and the church in this revival campaign. Those moments will come to be places of transfiguration before the month is over if you are faithful to that tryst with God.

Read about the revival every day. Not only read what you see about it in the newspaper, but be sure to look up in the calendar, as one of the first things you do in the morning, the text for each evening, and read as you have opportunity other selections from the Scriptures that are suggested to you by it.

Attend the meetings every day. I honestly believe that more than half of all the members of this church, with a reasonable amount of self-denial, giving no more devotion to it than they ordinarily give to business affairs, could attend every meeting in the revival series without missing a single service. It only requires that you shall make up your mind to do it. Set your heart on it, think of the great results that may come from it, remember that nobody pays so well as God does, and settle it that only a question of serious illness or solemn duty shall break your record of perfect attendance during the revival meetings. Cleveland never saw such a revival as we would have in this church if only half of our members should loyally and faithfully be in their place every night. There is a mighty power in that regular attendance. It gives God a fair chance to use you as a channel of divine communication to those who are not Christians.

It keeps you in touch with the spiritual atmosphere of the meetings and makes you available for effective work. It encourages the pastor more than anybody else can ever know. It cheers and inspires the other members of the church, and it convinces sinners of our interest and earnestness. It puts us on the ground where the battle is hottest, and offers opportunities to be useful in winning souls to Christ that never could come in any other way.

You can bear testimony to your faith and your purpose, if only by a Scripture quotation or a verse of a hymn, at every opportunity. What power would come to the meeting if you were all to do that! There is not a single member that ought to excuse himself from that. Jesus says, "Ye are my witnesses." If he were here on earth now, threatened with crucifixion again, how gladly we would bear our testimony for him. Yet by our silence we often "crucify the son of God afresh, and put him to an open shame." Let every one determine here and now that he will prepare in some way to bear witness to Christ at every chance he gets.

You can act promptly every time the pastor calls for Christians to gather at the altar for prayer or service. No other one thing, humanly speaking, would encourage the pastor, or the church, or impress unconverted people, more than that. And that is something that the one who feels humblest and most unworthy can do without fear. Make up your mind that you will never wait a moment for others when the pastor makes such a call. How my heart will burn within me with thanksgiving and hope if you heed this word!

You can speak or write every day to some unconverted persons about their personal attendance on the meetings and their personal salvation. This will not require any more thoughtfulness or fidelity than is required in ordinary business affairs. Most people are won to Christ by a personal invitation following up the influences of the pulpit. Let every member make a list of all the unconverted people he knows who live within the reach of the possible influence of these meetings. Make two copies of this list; keep one for yourself and bring one to me. It may take you a whole evening to do this, but you can not spend an evening better. If the list runs up into hundreds, no matter; let every one faithfully make this list, and then you and I will have somebody that we are definitely thinking about and praying for and seeking to save. That will give me a very large list; but by the help of God I will find some way of helping you to get into touch with them.

Invite somebody from this list, personally, every day, to attend the revival meetings. In order to be saved people must hear the Word; and it is just as important to get the people here as it is to preach to them right after they come.

Sing to the very best of your ability at every service. God gave you your voice to use for him, and you will never have a better chance to make return than during the revival meetings.

Every member of the church can lead in prayer, if only a single sentence, whenever called on. Who is there among us that could not say in public, leading the congregation, "God be merciful to me a sinner!" or, "Lord, I believe; help thou my unbelief!" or, "Revive thy work in our hearts!" or, "Forgive these souls who have sinned against thee, but now repent." I believe that many are kept from praying in public because the preacher and most members of the church who lead in prayer make too long prayers. I am going to set the example and enforce on others very brief petitions in public, so that if your prayer is very brief it will not seem unusual.

Be ready to speak a word of comfort and cheer to those who are seeking Christ. In fact, count yourself in and not out in everything that a Christian ought to do in worshiping God and in seeking lost souls and bringing them into the kingdom. In such harmony of action and spirit we may be sure that the Spirit of God will come upon us in great power, and multitudes will be saved.

L.
WHAT HAPPENS WHEN THERE IS A REVIVAL OF RELIGION.

Acts ii.

FIRST of all, there is an awakening of interest in spiritual things. Character seems more important than clothes, spiritual food more imperative than nourishment for the body, the life of the soul more glorious than the life of the flesh. Men pause in the rush and din of business to remember that they are only tenants at will in this world, and that they are hastening to a world where, for good or ill, for joy or sorrow, they are to dwell forever.

Prayer becomes vital and constant. It seems to be the natural breath of the soul. Christians not only say their prayers at certain times in the day, but they seem to realize Paul's wonderful exhortation in his letter to the Ephesians, to "pray without ceasing." Ever and anon through the days of revival Christian hearts will breathe out their prayer until the silent meditation is broken with words of prayer on the lips. Again and again, in times of revival, have I been awakened out of slumber at night with words of prayer the first vocal sounds I heard on my own tongue.

The Holy Spirit seems a real personality. Not some vague influence that works through chemical combination in giving shape and color to the flowers, or health to the atmosphere, or soothing to the troubled heart; but a loving personality with all the majesty of a father, with all the tenderness of a mother, with the persistent earnestness of the shepherd seeking out the lost sheep in the night. The Holy Spirit is honored and his presence expected and depended upon. The divine unction, which can not be exactly described in words, clothes the words of the preacher, and the testimonies of the people, and the tones of music, and gives to them all a pathos and a loving tenderness that nobody seems to understand the reason for, but which are mighty to break down the hard heart, arouse the sleeping conscience, and electrify the human will to determine and execute great things for righteousness.

The Bible comes to its rightful place as not only a great and important book, but The Book. Other books fall into insignificance for the time being, and the Bible reigns supreme. Christian people in their prayers voice snatches of thanksgiving from the Psalms, words of promise from the prophets and the apostles, figures of hope from the Master, and glimpses of glory from the seer of Patmos.

The old hymns come back to their kingdom. They no longer seem to be commonplace, but gather romance and dignity and commanding power. "Jesus, Lover of My Soul," "Rock of Ages, Cleft for Me," "A Charge to Keep I Have," "O Happy Day that Fixed My Choice," "Come, Ye Sinners, Poor and Needy," "Just as I Am, Without One Plea," "Nearer, My God, to Thee," "Oh, How Happy Are They," "There Is a Fountain Filled with Blood"—how these old hymns gather about them the freshness of immortal youth and awaken tears of glad appreciation as the heart is warmed and the memory quickened by divine fellowship!

An interest is aroused in the salvation of others. Suddenly Christians who have been going on quietly, honestly trying to do right, steadily seeking to be genuine and faithful, but after all thinking most of their own estate, see in the indifferent non-Christian men and women about them fellow immortals who are walking on the edge of a precipice, who are toying with eternal things, and who are in imminent danger of everlasting defeat. We are aroused to feel that our neighbors and their children, and possibly our own children, are taking care of the body but forgetting the soul. We have thought about it on ordinary days, but with comparative composure. It has not seemed the awful thing that it does now. Under the influence of this revived spiritual sensitiveness we see with clearer eyes, and appreciate, as we do not on ordinary occasions, what the absence of Christ from a soul means. We think with tears and anguish of what it must mean to live in this world with its sorrow, its disappointments, its dark and cheerless days, its unresting nights, its sickness, its separations, its forebodings of the future, without any hope in Christ to sustain the soul; with no Christ to whom we can breathe out the heart in lonely hours; no Christ upon whose bosom we may lay the aching head when facing misfortune; no Christ to lead us in the valley of shadows; no Christ to illuminate heaven for us in the vast beyond. The thought becomes impossible, horrible, to us, and with anxiety, with prayerfulness, with awakened love, we seek after the indifferent and the sinful, and entreat them to turn to Christ and be saved.

The dumb speak. Lips that have been silent in the prayer-meeting and in conversation concerning Christ and salvation break silence and speak glad words of praise to God and of entreaty to their fellow men. As on the day of Pentecost dependence was not put on Peter alone to effect the spiritual awakening of the people, but the one hundred and twenty men and women, many of them humble, ignorant, timid souls, went among the crowd and spoke to the people with such unction and earnestness that they said they heard every man in his own tongue the wonderful works of God, and thought there must be intoxication behind such marvelous zeal—so in a modern revival all the people preach. The minister's sermon is only one feature of the preaching of a revival. It only sets the key-note for the preaching that goes on in the homes, in the business houses, in the factories, in the pews—wherever an earnest man or woman, with heart aglow and lips touched with a coal from off the altar of God, urges sinners to repentance.

Finally, men and women turn from their sins. Consciences that have been hard and unfeeling are pricked to the quick; the Word of God is like a two-edged sword, so laying bare the sins of the people that aroused and conscience-stricken men and women cry out with fear and trembling, "What must I do to be saved?" And the minister and the church have an answer: "Believe on the Lord Jesus Christ, and thou shalt be saved." In that holy atmosphere men believe. With cleansing tears and open confession they surrender to Jesus Christ, and in the new sense of forgiveness and salvation that comes to them they rise up with shining faces and throbbing hearts to bear happy testimony that the burden has been lifted from their consciences and that their sins are all forgiven.

That is what happens when there is a revival of religion. God grant us such a revival!

LI.
A GREAT REVIVAL AND WHAT CAUSED IT.

2 Chronicles xx. 1-22.

IT is interesting to note, in the story of this great revival of genuine religion under Jehoshaphat and his chaplain Jahaziel, that the conditions were of the same sort that bring about a great religious revival in our own time. In the first place, a special time was set apart for the worship of God; not only for general worship, but a set time to implore the divine presence to be with them in giving them victory to a definite end. I heartily believe in the wisdom of setting apart a definite number of days and weeks for seeking the divine anointing for the winning of souls to Christ. God will honor our sacrifice in so doing, and we ourselves shall be thus able to bring our talents more completely to be used in that way. Such a setting apart of time by us will also attract the attention of those who are not Christians, and will impress upon their minds the fact that we are interested in them and are earnestly working for their personal salvation.

Another thing that I notice is that all the people came together—all the men, and their wives and their children, young and old, high and low, from the king down. The king himself made the first prayer. There is not a nation on earth that God would not mightily bless and save under those conditions. And we want those same conditions in our church work. If we are to have a great revival, the men of our church must so arrange their business that they can give daily attention to the revival meetings. Nothing must interfere with this month set apart for winning souls. We must have the men and the women and the children. If we will gather all our forces together, God will use us to his glory and to the salvation of multitudes of those who are going down to ruin without Christ. I hope we shall have the children just as much as possible in the revival meetings. It is a great loss every way, both for themselves and for others, to keep the children away from special evangelistic services. There is a tender and heavenly influence added by the presence of childhood in such meetings. Just as much as possible let us have the families brought together in this campaign for souls.

They depended on God. The meetings were largely prayer-meetings. They made a great deal of the singing; they sang of the beauty of holiness, and praised God for his mercy. We want to do all those things. They depended on the presence of the Holy Spirit to give power to the words of the preacher, and to lead and guide them. These causes brought about a great revival, and brought the people into such relation to God that he led them forth to wonderful victory. The same conditions will win in Cleveland now. They are the conditions antedating great revivals of religion in every age of the world.

I have been rereading the autobiography of Charles G. Finney, and I find that these were the simple conditions which always preceded the marvelous meetings which he held. He says that the spirit of prayer that prevailed in his revivals was a very marked feature of them. It was common for young converts to be greatly exercised in prayer; and in some instances so much so that they were constrained to continue in prayer whole nights, and until their bodily strength was quite exhausted, for the conversion of souls around them. There was a great pressure of the Holy Spirit upon the minds of Christians, and they seemed to bear about with them the burden of immortal souls. They manifested the greatest solemnity of mind, and the greatest watchfulness in all their words and actions. It was very common to find Christians, whenever they met in any place, instead of engaging in conversation, falling on their knees in prayer.

Not only were prayer-meetings greatly multiplied and fully attended, not only was there great solemnity in those meetings, but there was a mighty spirit of secret prayer. Christians prayed a great deal, many of them spending many hours in private prayer.

In regard to his own experience, Mr. Finney says that unless he had the spirit of prayer he could do nothing. If even for a day or an hour he lost the spirit of grace and supplication, he found himself unable to preach with power and efficiency, or to win souls by personal conversation.

I think it is of greatest importance that the supreme desire in regard to the revival meetings shall not be for our own good and our own happiness, but for the salvation of others. Mr. Finney relates this incident, which has impressed me very much: He was the guest of a gentleman who was one of the elders of the church, and the most intimate and influential friend of the minister. One day, as Mr. Finney came down from his room and was going out to call on some inquirers, he met his host in the hall, who said to him, "Mr. Finney, what would you think of a man that was praying week after week for the Holy Spirit, and could get no answer?" He replied that he should think he was praying from false motives. "But from what motives," said he, "should a man pray? If he wants to be happy, is that a false motive?" Finney replied, "Satan might pray with as good a motive as that;" and then quoted the words of the psalmist: "Uphold me with thy free spirit. Then will I teach transgressors thy ways, and sinners shall be converted unto thee." "See!" said Finney, "the psalmist did not pray for the Holy Spirit that he might be happy, but that he might be useful, and that sinners might be converted to Christ." This plain talk led to the man's honest seeking for salvation. He had never been really converted, but from that day he became an earnest and soul-winning Christian. Let us see to it that our motives are such as God can use and bless.

LII.
THE FIRST CHRISTMAS GIFTS.

Matthew ii.

THESE wise men were the students of the stars. They were men of reverent mind and holy life. They sought to find wisdom in the Milky Way and the sublime constellations of the heavens. They were men of a worshipful spirit. They saw God in the stars and revered him until their hearts were so sensitive to his presence that he was able to speak to them through the signal-light of the star in the East, which had no meaning to men of ruder mold and untaught heart. Following the signal of the skies, they made their journey across the deserts and sought with patient persistence until the star stood above the place where the child Christ lay in his mother's arms. Rich treasures were hidden in that caravan of camels, and these reverent astronomers brought forth their costly gifts of gold and frankincense and myrrh to lay at the feet of the little Babe.

It is a sublime picture. No wonder the poet

and the artist have ever regarded it as a fitting theme for their noblest work: the wisdom of the East bowing down at the feet of a little child; the wealth of the world poured out at the feet of a child so poor that its cradle was a manger. There is surely something worthy of our study in this old but ever new picture.

We are accustomed at Christmas-time to talk about Christmas from the divine side, the gift of God to the world in Jesus Christ. I would like to turn over the leaf and look at it from the other side. I believe it will be good for us to remember that the first Christmas gifts by men after the birth of Jesus were given to Christ himself. I do not believe it is healthful, morally, for us to always think about Christmas in the light of gifts made to us. It is not what we get in this world, but what we give, which measures and develops character. A man is judged not by the amount of wealth or learning or power which he achieves, but by what he does with it. He may use his power like Washington to advance liberty and bless humanity; or like Napoleon to feed his own selfishness, to the cost of suffering millions. He may use his wealth to advance art and science, to heal the sick through hospitals, to send the Gospel to the heathen, to relieve the poverty of the poor; or he may use it to feed his own greedy and miserly soul, until his name shall be cursed everywhere. A man may use learning to spread evil and vicious influences that blight like a simoom every mind and heart they blow upon; or he may use it to bring man closer to God, to give man power over nature, to heal his fellow men of the sorrows which come to them through ignorance. It is not what we get, but what we give, that marks the grade of humanity to which we belong.

There is something very comforting in this, for it puts our destiny in our own hands. We are not dependent on the generosity or support of other people. They may give or withhold their approbation; they can not, if they would, restrain the growth of nobility in us. Greatness in character is graded by service. It is not how many people it takes to take care of me, but how many people I can take care of, how many burdens I can carry, how many hearts I can cheer, how many tears I can banish, how much joy I can bring to the world, that measures the quality of the man to which I belong. Surely this is a good thing for us to think about on Christmas-time.

I think it will be well for us to study briefly the gifts which these wise scholars of the Orient brought to the infant Christ. First, they brought their gold. Gold is business life condensed. In that day it meant caravans, herds, flocks, and raiment, as to-day it means railroads, steamships, and houses. The commercial life of the world is civilized by gold. In that broad sense we ought, this Christmas-time, to lay our business at the feet of Jesus Christ. A man has no right to a kind of business that he can not bring confidently to Jesus and submit to the perfect innocence of Christ's gaze. Our business is not our own. We can not separate it from our religious lives. We have no right to separate our lives into water-tight compartments like a modern ship, and call one domestic, and another religious, and another financial—to call one secular and another spiritual. Life is a unit. Character is a unit. Failure at one point works ruin everywhere. The whole life should be consecrated to Christ, and we can not separate our business life from the rest. If we are Christians we must do business in the Christian spirit, and we must hold our business, our substance, our gold at the call of Jesus, who is our King.

And there is the frankincense. This was one of the main ingredients in the making of incense which was used in offering sacrifices to God in public worship. It suggests the thought of worship. We should bring our worship to Jesus Christ. We should crown him Lord over all in our hearts. "The gift without the giver is bare." We should live reverent lives. A mere ceremony however splendid, or a gift of gold however rich, is mockery if the frankincense of a reverent spirit which admires, adores, loves, worships Christ is lacking in our hearts.

Then there is the myrrh. I do not agree with some commentators who make this signify only the fact that Christ was to die, and to suggest the thought of the embalming of his body. True, myrrh was used in embalming the dead; but it was also used as an ingredient in making the holy oil, and was a very rare and grateful perfume. It seems, therefore, to me that it far more clearly suggests to us the thought of sweetness and fragrance and beauty. I do not believe for a moment that these wise men from the East brought their rich treasures of myrrh, the most delicious of perfumes, to lay at the feet of the babe Christ with reference to his dying, but rather with reference to his living; with thought about his childhood, his youth, his beauty, his purity, his strength, his kingliness of character. It suggests to me that we ought to bring to Christ our pleasures and our joys. We ought to bring him all the beautiful things of our lives. We shall not lose them by bringing them to Christ. When he was on earth the social circle at the wedding feast was all the more joyous because Christ was there, and our social life and all our feasts of enjoyment will grow in richness and significance if Jesus honors them by his presence. On this Christmas day we should lay all our joys and pleasures at the feet of Jesus for his blessing. Any pleasure that will wither in the sight of his eyes would poison us, and every wholesome joy will gain in power and gladness with his benediction upon it.

Books by 🍀 🍀
DR. LOUIS ALBERT BANKS.

Christ and His Friends.

A Collection of Revival Sermons, Simple and Direct, and Wholly Devoid of Oratorical Artifice, but Rich in Natural Eloquence, and Burning with Spiritual Fervor. The author has strengthened and enlivened them with many illustrations and anecdotes. 12mo, Cloth, Gilt Top, Rough Edges. Price, $1.50; post-free.

National Presbyterian, Indianapolis: "One of the most marked revivals attended their delivery, resulting in hundreds of conversions. Free from extravagance and fantasticism, in good taste, dwelling upon the essentials of religious faith, their power has not been lost in transference to the printed page."

New York Observer: "These sermons are mainly hortatory . . . always aiming at conviction or conversion. They abound in fresh and forcible illustrations. . . . They furnish a fine specimen of the best way to reach the popular ear, and may be commended as putting the claims of the Gospel upon men's attention in a very direct and striking manner. No time is wasted in rhetorical ornament, but every stroke tells upon the main point."

The Fisherman and His Friends.

A Companion Volume to "Christ and His Friends," consisting of Thirty-one Stirring Revival Discourses, full of Stimulus and Suggestion for Ministers, Bible class Teachers, and all Christian Workers and Others who Desire to become Proficient in the Supreme Capacity of Winning Souls to Christ. They furnish a rich store of fresh spiritual inspiration, their subjects being strong, stimulating, and novel in treatment, without being sensational or elaborate. They were originally preached by the author in a successful series of revival meetings, which resulted in many conversions. 12mo, Cloth, Gilt Top. Price, $1.50; post-free.

Bishop John F. Hurst: "It is a most valuable addition to our devotional literature."

New York Independent: "There is no more distinguished example of the modern people's preacher in the American pulpit to-day than Dr. Banks. *This volume fairly thrills and rocks with the force injected into its utterance.*"

BOOKS BY DR. LOUIS ALBERT BANKS—Continued.

The People's Christ.

A Volume of Sermons and Other Addresses and Papers. 12mo, Cloth, $1.25.

New York Observer: "These sermons are excellent specimens of discourses adapted to reach the masses. Their manner of presenting Christian truth is striking. They abound in all kinds of illustration, and are distinguished by a bright, cheerful tone and style, which admirably fit them for making permanent impression."

Heavenly Trade-Winds.

A Volume of Sermons. 12mo, Cloth, $1.25.

From author's preface: "The sermons included in this volume have all been delivered in the regular course of my ministry in the Hanson-Place Methodist Episcopal Church, Brooklyn. They have been blessed of God in confronting the weary, giving courage to the faint, arousing the indifferent, and awakening the sinful."

The Honeycombs of Life.

A Volume of Sermons. 12mo, Cloth, $1.50.

Most of the discourses are spiritual honeycombs, means of refreshment and illumination by the way. "The Soul's Resources," "Cure for Anxiety," "At the Beautiful Gate," "The Pilgrimage of Faith," and "Wells in the Valley of Baca," are among his themes. The volume is well laden with evangelical truth, and breathes a holy inspiration. This volume also includes Dr. Banks's Memorial tribute to Lucy Stone and his powerful sermon in regard to the Chinese in America, entitled "Our Brother in Yellow."

Immortal Hymns and Their Story.

The Narrative of the Conception and Striking Experiences of Blessing Attending the Use of some of the World's Greatest Hymns. With 21 Portraits and 25 full-page half-tone illustrations by NORVAL JORDAN. 8vo, Cloth, Gilt Top, $3.00.

An Oregon Boyhood.

The story of Dr. Banks's boyhood in Oregon in the pioneer days, including innumerable dramatic, romantic, and exciting experiences of frontier life. 12mo, Cloth. Tastefully bound and printed. Illustrated. Price $1.25.

FUNK & WAGNALLS COMPANY, Publishers, NEW YORK and LONDON

BOOKS BY DR. LOUIS ALBERT BANKS—Continued.

Seven Times Around Jericho.

Seven Strong and Stirring Temperance Discourses, in which Deep Enthusiasm is Combined with Rational Reasoning—A Refreshing Change from the Conventional Temperance Arguments. Pathetic incidents and stories are made to carry most convincingly their vital significance to the subjects discussed. They treat in broad manner various features of the question. 12mo, Handsomely Bound in Polished Buckram. Price, 75 cents.

Herald and Presbyter, Cincinnati: "The book is sure to be a power for good. The discourses have the true ring."

Jersey City News: "Such able discourses as these of Dr. Banks will wonderfully help the great work of educating and arousing the people to their duty."

Revival Quiver.

A Pastor's Record of Four Revival Campaigns. 12mo, Cloth, $1.50.

This book is, in some sense, a record of personal experiences in revival work. It begins with "Planning for a Revival," followed by "Methods in Revival Work." This is followed by brief outlines of some hundred or more sermons. They have points to them, and one can readily see that they were adapted to the purpose designed. The volume closes with "A Scheme of City Evangelization." It seems to us a valuable book, adapted to the wants of many a preacher and pastor.

White Slaves; or, The Oppression of the Worthy Poor.

Fifty Illustrations. 12mo, Cloth, $1.50.

The Rev. Dr. Banks has made a personal and searching investigation into the homes of the poorer classes, and in the "White Slaves" the results are given. The work is illustrated from photographs taken by the author; and the story told by pen and camera is startling. It should be borne in mind that the author's visits were made to the homes of the worthy poor, who are willing to work hard for subsistence, and not to the homes of the criminal and vicious.

The Christ Dream.

12mo, Cloth, $1.20.

A series of twenty-four sermons in which illustrations of the Christ ideal are thrown upon the canvas, showing here and there individuals who have risen above the selfish, and measure up to the Christ dream. In tone it is optimistic, and sees the bright side of life.

Common Folks' Religion.

A Volume of Sermons. 12mo, Cloth, $1.50.

Boston Journal: "Dr. Banks presents Christ to the 'common people,' and preaches to every-day folk the glorious every-day truths of the Scripture. The sermons are original, terse, and timely, full of reference to current topics, and have that earnest quality which is particularly needed to move the people for whom they were spoken."

BOOKS BY DR. LOUIS ALBERT BANKS — Continued.

Paul and His Friends.

A companion volume to "Christ and His Friends," and "The Fisherman and His Friends," being similarly bound and arranged. The book contains thirty-one stirring revival sermons delivered in a special series of revival services at the First M. E. Church, Cleveland. 12mo, Cloth, Gilt Top, Rough Edges. Price, $1.50.

The Christian Gentleman.

A volume of original and practical addresses to young men. The addresses were originally delivered to large and enthusiastic audiences of men, in Cleveland, at the Young Men's Christian Association Hall. 12mo, Buckram. Price, 75 cents.

Hero Tales from Sacred Story.

The Romantic Stories of Bible Characters Retold in Graphic Style, with Modern Parallels and Striking Applications. Richly Illustrated with 19 Full-page, Half-tone Illustrations from Famous Paintings. 12mo, Cloth, Gilt Top, Cover Design by George Wharton Edwards. Price, $1.50.

Christian Work, New York: "One can not imagine a better book to put into the hands of a young man or young woman than this."

The Saloon-Keeper's Ledger.

The Business and Financial Side of the Drink Question. Among the items treated are: The Saloon Debtor to Disease, Private and Social Immorality, Ruined Homes, Lawlessness and Crime, and Political Corruption. 12mo, Cloth. Price, 75 cents.

The Christian Herald, Detroit: "This is one of the most notable contributions to temperance literature of recent years. The discourses are the masterpieces of an expert, abounding in apt illustrations and invincible logic, sparkling with anecdote, and scintillating with unanswerable facts."

Sermon Stories for Boys and Girls.

Short Stories of great interest, with which are interwoven lessons of practical helpfulness for young minds. The stories have been previously told in the author's congregation, where their potency and attractiveness have become surprisingly manifest. The book has a special value for the Sunday-school, the nursery, the pastor's study, and the school-room. 12mo, Cloth, Artistic Cover Design, Illustrated. Price, $1.00.

www.ingramcontent.com/pod-product-compliance
Lightning Source LLC
Chambersburg PA
CBHW022112230426
43672CB00008B/1357